The WRONGFUL CONVICTION

of OSCAR PISTORIUS

Science Transforms
our Comprehension
of Reeva Steenkamp's
Shocking Death

Brent Willock, Ph.D.

Torchflame Books
An imprint of Light Messages
Durham, NC

The Wrongful Conviction of Oscar Pistorius: Science Transforms our Comprehension of Reeva Steenkamp's Shocking Death

Published 2018, by Torchflame Books
an Imprint of Light Messages
www.lightmessages.com
Durham, NC 27713 USA
SAN: 920-9298

Paperback ISBN: 978-1-61153-267-8
E-book ISBN: 978-1-61153-268-5
Library of Congress Control Number: 2018938633

PRAISE FOR THIS BOOK FROM LEADING AUTHORITIES IN THE SCIENTIFIC AND FORENSIC FIELDS

This book is a murder mystery but not a 'who done it?' We know who fired the shots through the door of the toilet room killing Reeva, the girlfriend of Oscar Pistorius. He had been asleep next to her when he was awakened by a noise he thought was due to one or more intruders. He ran to the bathroom calling to Reeva to phone the police and shouting to the intruder(s) to get out of his house. Neither she nor they responded. After being frozen in fear he shot through the locked door and then discovered Reeva close to death. From here on the story is a detailed analysis of the legal procedures, the misunderstandings of the state of mind of the accused: was he fully conscious and so responsible for murder? The author, Brent Willock, is highly informed to make a compelling case that Oscar was not fully conscious, therefore not responsible, and to address the other possible states of mind Oscar may have gone through during and following this tragic event. The book sums up the pressing need for lawyers, judges and jurors to become familiar with the unconscious mind of sleep that does not obey the logic of the mind fully awake.

—Rosalind Cartwright, Ph.D. Professor and Chairman Emerita, Department of Behavioral Sciences and Director, Sleep Disorder Center, Rush University Medical Center, Chicago. Author, *The Twenty-four Hour Mind: the role of sleep and dreaming in our emotional lives* (Oxford University Press).

This well-researched, scientifically accurate, and nicely written book by Dr. Willock invokes an alternative explanation for Oscar Pistorius' behaviors on February 14, 2013, namely that the tragic event could be well-explained by a parasomnia (confusional arousal/sleepwalking). Such conditions are a reminder that wake and sleep are not mutually exclusive, but rather may co-exist simultaneously: part of the brain capable of producing complex behaviors is awake, while parts responsible for monitoring and laying down memories of such behaviors are asleep permitting behavior without conscious awareness and therefore without culpability. Furthermore, during these states of mixed wake and sleep, there may be impaired perception of the environment with diminished insight, judgement, and reasoning resulting in flawed recall of details of these events which may appear unrealistic, puzzling, confusing, contradictory, unreasonable, or irrational. This scientifically-based concept should be valuable to all parties (perpetrator, victim, prosecution, and defense) in future similar cases.

—Mark W. Mahowald, MD, Professor of Neurology, University of Minnesota Medical School, Minneapolis, MN, USA (Retired)

—Michel A. Cramer Bornemann, MD, D-ABSM, FAASM, Lead Investigator—Sleep Forensics Associates (SFA)

DEDICATED TO

Wenchang Wang (文昌王), also known as
Wenchang Dijun (文昌帝君)
Taoist God of Culture and Literature

———✳———

Ganesha & Saraswati
Hindu patron deities of writers

———✳———

The Muses
Greek inspirational goddesses of literature,
science, and the arts

———✳———

And all others who inspire us to put pen to paper
in hopes of contributing to the evolution of
human understanding

DEDICATED TO

Wenchang Wang (文昌王), also known as
Wenchang Dijun (文昌帝君)
Taoist God of Culture and Literature

Ganesha & Saraswati
Hindu patron deities of writers

The Muses,
Greek/Roman mythical goddesses of literature,
science, and the arts

...all others who inspire us to put pen to paper,
in hopes of contributing to the evolution of
human understanding

vi

Contents

ACKNOWLEDGEMENTS

I approached three of the most eminent persons in the scientific field from which I draw in this book to see if they might be interested in reading my manuscript. Not only are they highly accomplished scientists-clinicians but they are also leading forensic authorities in this area. They have provided expert opinions to many courts in similarly complex cases. Apart from my familiarity with their enormous contributions to the scientific, professional, and forensic literatures, I have never met any of these individuals. They do not know me. I was delighted to discover that they were all very interested in the project I had outlined to them. Despite their extremely busy schedules, they were eager to read the manuscript and, ultimately, to generously endorse it. For their marvellous support, I am extremely grateful. I extend my profound thanks to Dr. Michel Cramer Bornemann, Dr. Mark Mahowald, and Dr. Rosalind Cartwright.

The fine cover photograph of Oscar Pistorius at his bail hearing in the Pretoria Magistrate Court on February 20, 2013 was taken by Herman Verwey who is associated with Gallo Images and City Press. This photograph is reprinted courtesy of Creative Commons and Flickr (CC BY 2.0).

Many thanks to Elizabeth Turnbull, Senior Editor at Light Messages Publishing, for creating a superb book cover in relation to the preceding photograph.

I am grateful to Creative Commons and to all the photographers who have given their pictures to the Commons, permitting them to be utilized by those of us who work in words, images, and ideas. I am especially thankful to Elvar Pálsson, Michael Greenwood, and Frennie Shivambu whose photographs I have reprinted in this book. I believe their works truly are worth a thousand words.

It has been a great pleasure to collaborate closely with my publisher, Walter Turnbull, over the past many months. He is an outstanding exemplar of the enormous cultural value, creativity, and resourcefulness of small, independent book publishers. He (and they) have and continue to enrich our literary landscape enormously.

Finally I want to thank my many friends, family members, and colleagues for their ongoing support of this endeavor. Here I can only mention a few who were especially helpful and encouraging: Liz Chin-Sam; Bob, Sherrill, and Graham Willard; Edward Davidson; Robert Halpin; Laura Bass; Denise Bukowski; Hazel Ipp; Marilyn Willock; Mark Egit; Keith Haartman; Judi Kubrick; Florence Loh; and Dagnija Tenne. My heartfelt gratitude to you all!

PART I

Inauspicious Beginnings, Glorious Middle, and Then ...

Chapter 1

WHO IS OSCAR PISTORIUS?

If we all worked on the assumption that what is accepted as true is really true, there would be little hope of advance.
—Orville Wright

How things can change! Completely. Unexpectedly. Drastically. In a flash.

For several years prior to the blindsiding events of February 14, 2013, Oscar Pistorius had been the subject of intense international fascination and admiration. For a few years after that awful night, the world continued to follow his life story with equal enthralment. Now, however, the citizenry's absorption was of a far less exuberant sort. During both these time periods, virtually everyone knew of this extraordinary man. He had burst into our collective consciousness like a dazzling lightning bolt from Planet Earth's southern hemisphere. Just a few years later, many are already beginning to forget his uniquely inspiring, and equally shocking story. Yesterday my neighbor asked what I am writing about. When I answered, he responded, "Who is Oscar Pistorius?" I must thank him for providing the title and topic for this opening chapter.

Transitioning from intense engagement with Oscar to increasing amnesia, we are in danger in this, and so many other instances, of learning little of lasting value. Contra that corrosive current, this book aims to enable us to acquire and retain important insights from the devastating downturn in this hitherto celebrated life. Knowledge gained from carefully exploring profoundly puzzling, key evidence from his ordeal from an entirely new perspective will empower us to, at last, make sense of this terrible tragedy. What we will discover by radically re-considering crucial testimony will be fascinating and helpful not only to the hitherto entranced public, reeling from the one hundred and eighty degree turn in this Olympic athlete's life story, but also to the legal system charged with comprehending these and future events of similarly mind-boggling magnitude. All that we will learn during this voyage of discovery will facilitate both individual and social healing.

From Womb to World Stage

Born on November 22, 1986 in Johannesburg, South Africa, Oscar Leonard Carl Pistorius was raised in a religious, Christian home with his older brother, Carl, and younger sister, Aimée. Unlucky in utero, he set foot—grossly deformed feet—on our planet with fibular hemimelia in both legs (absence of the fibula, the outer, thinner of the two bones that extend from knee to foot). His ankles were only half-formed. His heels faced sideways. Instead of five toes, he had two. Realizing no human being could ever stand, let alone walk on such narrow, twisted, incompletely formed feet, his parents consulted nearly a dozen doctors. These specialists' recommendations ranged from years of complex surgeries to immediate, bilateral amputations. Who could feel anything but intense sympathy for this infant and his family as they struggled to make the best of their difficult situation?

Shortly before Oscar's first birthday—the time when babies normally begin to walk—his lower legs were cut off, halfway between his knees and ankles. The surgeon transplanted Oscar's heel pads to the remaining stumps, hoping to facilitate his learning to walk. Three months later, fitted with artificial legs, baby Oscar took his first uncertain steps. Despite frequent stumbles, like all toddlers he relished his new locomotor ability.

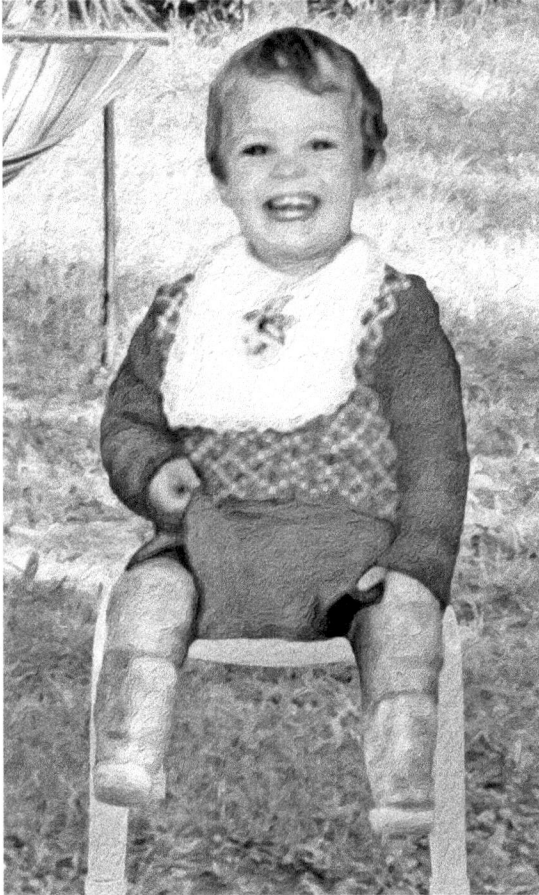

By W. Turnbull CC by 2.0
Digital painting of toddler Oscar

As Oscar grew up, his mother encouraged him to not define himself as disabled. Absorbing her determinedly positive perspective, he learned to run, play games, and ride mountain bikes, usually with his brother, Carl. In these exuberant pursuits that included climbing and falling off trees, he always picked himself up from any mishaps and got right back into the adventure.

When Oscar was six years old, he was struck by yet another challenge. His parents divorced. The familiar world that had held, nourished, and sustained him since time immemorial shattered. His father, Henke, moved seven hundred miles away. His mother, Sheila, relocated with her children to a less expensive, rougher neighborhood where they suffered several break-ins. She went to work, further transforming the universe her offspring had known and, incorrectly, assumed would go on being like it had been.

After finishing primary school, blessed with a well-to-do uncle, Oscar was afforded the opportunity of becoming a boarder at the Pretoria Boys High School. Notable alumni from this storied institution included two Nobel Prize laureates, eighteen Rhodes scholars, several government ministers and members of parliament, eight judges of the Supreme Court of Appeal, and numerous prominent intellectuals and sportsmen. Perhaps surprisingly, Oscar's talents proved to be in that latter category. Embracing vigorous physical challenges and competition, he signed up for his school's rugby team, wrestled, played water polo, participated in tennis at the provincial level, and trained at a local gym. He became part of school folklore when, during a rugby match, a player from the opposite team tackled him. Oscar's legs came off in the boy's arms, but he carried on, running over the line.

Despite Oscar's positive adaptation to very challenging circumstances, his situation was far from easy. He was prone to developing painful sores and blisters on his leg stumps. For stretches of several months he could barely move, let alone walk. To heal, he had to stay home with his mother, separated from school and friends.

In June 2003, while playing rugby, Oscar suffered a serious knee injury. While undergoing rehabilitative procedures at the University of Pretoria's High Performance Centre, he was introduced to a safer sport: running. Acquiring his first racing blades, he trained diligently and began participating in Paralympic events. Bravely embodying his mother's can-do philosophy, he soon set new world records.

Photo by Elvar Pálsson CC by 2.0

July 8, 2007. Oscar takes part in Iceland's largest sporting event which is held every three years.

Next, with the support of a pair of J-shaped, carbon-fiber prosthetics (evocatively called "Flex-Foot Cheetahs"), Oscar took a quantum leap to the next phase of his athletic odyssey. He began competing against *able-bodied* runners. Soon he became known and admired around the world. His fans affectionately bestowed upon him a variety of affectionate nicknames such as the Blade Runner, Oz, and the Fastest Man On No Legs.

Some upset, highly vocal critics claimed Oscar's artificial limbs gave him an unfair advantage over able-bodied athletes. Responding to those complaints on March 26, 2007, the International Association of Athletics Federations (IAAF) banned the use of any technical device that "provides a user with an advantage over another athlete not using such a device." Their amendment was not specifically aimed at Oscar, they said. The IAFF invited the Blade Runner to undergo tests at Cologne Sports University to ascertain whether his Cheetahs provided an unfair edge. Oscar travelled to Germany for that evaluation where Dr. Peter Brüggemann, Professor of Biomechanics, concluded that the Flex-Foot Cheetahs gave considerable advantages. Consequently, the IAAF declared these prostheses could not be used in competitions conducted under their rules.

Never one to give up in when faced with adversity, Oscar appealed the IAAF decision to the Court of Arbitration for Sport (CAS) in Lausanne, Switzerland. The CAS found flaws in Professor Brüggemann's methodology. He had only tested Oscar's biomechanics when he was running in a straight line—unlike real 400-metre races that feature multiple curvatures. Furthermore, Professor Brüggemann had not taken into consideration the disadvantages Oscar suffers at the start and acceleration phases of races. The CAS concluded there was no evidence suggesting he had any net advantage over able-bodied athletes. Consequently, the IAAF decision was revoked.

Responding to this good news, Oscar stated: "My focus throughout this appeal has been to ensure that disabled athletes be given the chance to compete and compete fairly with able-bodied athletes." Free from the frustration of the earlier IAAF decision, he could now continue pursuing his dream: the upcoming 2012 (*able-bodied*) Olympics in London. On July 19, 2011 Oscar achieved his personal best time in the 400-meter race, resulting in his being ranked as the 15th fastest runner in the world in this event. In recognition of this achievement, he was awarded the World Championships and Olympic Games "A" qualification, enabling him to enter the World Championships in Daegu, South Korea. There, he became the first double amputee to ever win an able-bodied world track medal.

The following year, Oscar became the first amputee to ever compete at the Olympic Games. Proudly he carried South Africa's flag for the closing ceremony in London. In the ensuing Paralympics, he was again selected to carry his nation's flag, this time for the opening ceremony. The Blade Runner was now one of the most famous, most respected athletes in the world.

Awestruck people everywhere realized they were privileged to be witnessing a remarkable individual's historic triumph over congenital hardship. In recognition of his accomplishments, in 2007 Oscar received the British Broadcasting Corporation's Sports Personality of the Year Helen Rollason Award. This honor is conferred on a small number of individuals who have shown outstanding courage and achievement in the face of adversity. The next year, he was included in *Time* magazine's annual list of the world's most influential people. In 2012, Glasgow's University of Strathclyde bestowed an honorary doctorate. Oscar praised that institution for leading the way in prosthetic research and development. After the ceremony, he met with dedicated staff and grateful patients at their pioneering National Centre for Prosthetics and Orthotics.

Photo by Michael Greenwood CC by 2.0

August 29, 2012. Oscar proudly leads the South African Paralympic Team in the Opening Ceremonies in London.

Outside his passionate athletic pursuits, Oscar began studying for a Bachelor of Commerce degree at the University of Pretoria in 2006. Two years later, his autobiography, *Dream Runner*, was published in Italy, a country to which he had ancestral connections and where he trained athletically. The English version of that book, *Blade Runner,* was released the following year. In 2008, he cut a musical CD, *Olympic Dream*. Also produced in Italy, it consisted of remixes of pieces he found inspirational, supplemented by two tracks written especially for him for which he provided voiceovers. Part of this project's proceeds was given to charity.

Admired for his astounding accomplishments, generosity, charm, handsome appearance, and winning personality, in 2010 Oscar appeared on *L'isola dei famosi*, an Italian version of *Celebrity Survivor*. Two years later, he danced a tango with Annalisa Longo to the renowned Swedish pop group ABBA's song, *The Winner Takes It All* on Italian television's version of *Dancing with the Stars* (*Ballando con le Stelle*).

Sponsored by Nike, Oakley, British Telecommunications, Thierry Mugler, and Össur (an Icelandic manufacturer of prosthetic devices), he participated in numerous activities to raise funds for people in difficult circumstances. He joined celebrity charity golfing tournaments, donated speaking fees to benevolent organizations, and supported the Mineseeker Foundation, a charity that raises awareness of the horrors of landmines and provides prosthetic equipment for victims of those diabolical devices. He helped children who, like himself, lacked limbs and were trying to make their way in the world with artificial ones. He inspired these youngsters to believe that they, too, with support, could bravely face and transcend their challenging situations.

Getty Images photo by Liza van Deventer

A four-year-old South African double amputee spends time with his hero, Oscar Pistorius, at the Olympic athlete's home on November 24, 2011.

Chapter 2

THE SAINT VALENTINE'S DAY MASSACRE

Every human being suffers from some wound, visible or invisible, and given to him at birth. The grandeur in some individuals lies in their striving to overcome this congenital blight or, failing that, to compensate for it.

—Irving Layton,
Waiting for the Messiah

Pretoria, South Africa: In the early morning hours of February 14, 2013, Oscar Leonard Carl Pistorius pressed the trigger on his 9 mm Parabellum pistol. In swift succession, four powerful bullets penetrated the wooden door to the toilet chamber in his home in the Silver Woods Country Estate. On the other side of that divide, his girlfriend, law school graduate and fashion model, Reeva Steenkamp, now lay dead. Overwhelmed with shock and grief, Oscar immediately acknowledged responsibility. Devastated, he explained that in the darkness of the night, he had mistakenly thought Reeva was a home invader. As this horrific news spread around the world, millions of people could scarcely believe what they were hearing. Surely it could not possibly be true that this hitherto so uplifting, transformative story had crashed precipitously, shattering to pieces in one sickening instant.

Detective Hilton Botha, a hardened veteran of countless homicide investigations, told Mark Seal, a journalist for *Vanity Fair,* that he had immediately conceptualized this case as being commonplace and simple. In South Africa, "intimate femicide" is the leading cause of women's violent deaths. One woman is killed by her husband, boyfriend, or same-sex partner every eight hours. In the year that Reeva Steenkamp died, more than one thousand other women's lives were obliterated by their partners. "There is no way anything else could have happened," declared Botha. "It was just them in the house. ...There was no forced entry. The only place there could have been entrance was the open bathroom window, and we did everything we could to see if anyone went through it, and it was impossible. So I thought it was an open-and-closed case. ...I was convinced that it was murder." Accordingly, Oscar was arrested and promptly transported to a Pretoria police station.

The day she died, Reeva, a feminist and devout Christian, had been scheduled to deliver a speech against gender violence to students at a Johannesburg school. Statistics she posted on Twitter showed that in South Africa a woman is raped every four minutes. In her talk, she had planned to reveal to the students that she had once been in an abusive relationship. She wanted to urge girls not to put up with mistreatment.

The next stage in Oscar's legal proceedings involved the event being classified as a Schedule 6 crime—premeditated murder. This appellation constituted major victory for the prosecution. In face of such classification, if Oscar hoped to be released on bail, he would have to prove that "exceptional circumstances" needed to be taken into consideration. To avoid spending up to two years in prison awaiting trial, he presented an affidavit providing his perspective on what had transpired that terrible night:

On the 13th of February 2013 Reeva would have gone out with her friends and I with my friends. Reeva then called me and asked that we rather spend the evening at home.

I agreed and we were content to have a quiet dinner together at home. By about 22h00 on 13 February 2013 we were in our bedroom. She was doing her yoga exercises and I was in bed watching television.

My prosthetic legs were off. We were deeply in love and I could not be happier. I know she felt the same way. She had given me a present for Valentine's Day but asked me only to open it the next day. After Reeva finished her yoga exercises she got into bed and we both fell asleep.

I am acutely aware of violent crime being committed by intruders entering homes with a view to commit crime, including violent crime. I have received death threats before. I have also been a victim of violence and of burglaries before. For that reason I kept my firearm, a 9 mm Parabellum, underneath my bed when I went to bed at night.

During the early morning hours of 14 February 2013, I woke up, went onto the balcony to bring the fan in and closed the sliding doors, the blinds and the curtains. I heard a noise in the bathroom and realized that someone was in the bathroom. I felt a sense of terror rushing over me. There are no burglar bars across the bathroom window and I knew that contractors who worked at my house had left the ladders outside.

Although I did not have my prosthetic legs on I have mobility on my stumps. I believed that someone had entered my house. I was too scared to switch a light on. I grabbed my 9mm pistol from underneath my bed. On my way to the bathroom I screamed words to the effect for him/them to get out of my house and for Reeva to phone the police. It was pitch dark in the bedroom and I thought Reeva was in bed.

I noticed that the bathroom window was open. I realized that the intruder/s was/were in the toilet because the toilet door was closed and I did not see anyone in the bathroom. I heard movement inside the toilet. The toilet is inside the bathroom and has a separate door. It filled me with horror and fear of an intruder or intruders being inside the toilet.

I thought he or they must have entered through the unprotected window. As I did not have my prosthetic legs on and felt extremely vulnerable, I knew I had to protect Reeva and myself. I believed that when the intruder/s came out of the toilet we would be in grave danger.

I felt trapped as my bedroom door was locked and I have limited mobility on my stumps. I fired shots at the toilet door and shouted to Reeva to phone the police. She did not respond and I moved backwards out of the bathroom, keeping my eyes on the bathroom entrance. Everything was pitch dark in the bedroom and I was still too scared to switch on a light. Reeva was not responding. When I reached the bed, I realized that Reeva was not in bed.

That is when it dawned on me that it could have been Reeva who was in the toilet. I returned to the bathroom calling her name. I tried to open the toilet door but it was locked. I rushed back into the bedroom and opened the sliding door exiting onto the balcony and screamed for help. I put on my prosthetic legs, ran back to the bathroom and tried to kick the toilet door open. I think I must then have turned on the lights.

I went back into the bedroom and grabbed my cricket bat to bash open the toilet door. A panel or panels broke off and I found the key on the floor and unlocked and opened the door. Reeva was slumped over but alive. I battled to get her out of the toilet and pulled her into the bathroom.

I phoned Johan Stander ("Stander") who was involved in the administration of the estate and asked him to phone the ambulance. I phoned Netcare and asked for help. I went downstairs to open the front door. I returned to the bathroom and picked Reeva up as I *had* been told not to wait for the paramedics, but to take her to hospital. I carried her downstairs in order to take her to the hospital. On my way down Stander arrived.

A doctor who lives in the complex also arrived. Downstairs, I tried to render the assistance to Reeva that I could, but she died in my arms. I am absolutely mortified by the events and the devastating loss of my beloved Reeva. With the benefit of hindsight I believe that Reeva went to the toilet when I went out on the balcony to bring the fan in.

I cannot bear to think of the suffering I have caused her and her family, knowing how much she was loved. I also know that the events of that tragic night were as I have described them and that in due course I have no doubt the police and expert investigators will bear this out. ...I maintain good relationships with people and I bear no grudges against anyone. ...I have no previous convictions. ...I am not disposed to violence. ...I do not constitute a flight risk. ...After the shooting I did not attempt to flee. Rather, I accepted Stander would contact the police, and I remained at the scene. ...I respectfully submit that should I be released on bail, my release shall not disturb the public order or undermine the proper functioning of the criminal justice system. I will comply with such conditions as the above Honourable Court may wish to impose. I accordingly submit that the interests of justice, considerations of prejudice and the balancing of respective interests favour my release on bail.

After extensive deliberations, Bail Magistrate Desmond Nair pronounced that Oscar's application to be released on bail was reasonable, subject to the condition that he must reside with his uncle.

In just one moment, Oscar's meteoric ascent to Olympic accomplishment, international fame and admiration had collapsed precipitously. These explosive events left behind a bloody corpse, an emotionally distraught boyfriend, devastated families and friends, and millions of people in every country reeling in shock, disbelief, outrage, and dismay. The Fastest Man On No Legs' years of disciplined, dedicated determination to overcome major challenges in order to create the best life he possibly could had hit a stone cold wall. His story that had so moved and inspired persons throughout the world now had a radically opposite, equally powerful, but profoundly disheartening impact.

The judicial system was faced with the challenging task of examining evidentiary details to make sense of this catastrophe, endeavoring to reach a just decision. Meanwhile, people debated intensely as to whether the athlete's or the police version of events was true. The world argued heatedly and held its collective breath.

Chapter 3

TRIAL AND JUDGEMENT

Like the police, prosecuting attorney Gerrie Nel believed Oscar had intentionally murdered Reeva in a fit of lover's rage. Nel summoned several of the Blade Runner's neighbors to give evidence supporting this theory. Some claimed they had heard the couple quarrelling during the night in question. A few recalled having heard a woman screaming before the four fatal shots were fired. The state argued that Reeva, feeling threatened as their quarrel escalated, locked herself in the bathroom to protect herself from her enraged lover. Pursuing her with his gun, swept up in a tsunami of anger, Oscar deliberately terminated her life. To exonerate himself, he concocted his story about having mistaken her for a burglar. Under South African law, murder requires a minimum sentence of fifteen years unless special circumstances warrant a lesser consequence.

After months of testimony, cross examination, and expert witnesses, Judge Thokozile Matilda Masipa concluded that Oscar's version of events (that he had simply made a horrific mistake) was credible, apart from some glaringly incomprehensible elements. She felt he had been, and continued to be genuinely shocked and remorseful about his fatal error. Assuming he was trying to protect himself and Reeva from intruders, he should, nevertheless, not have pursued a course of action likely to cause death, Judge

Masipa averred. He should have fired a warning shot, fled, or called the building's security personnel or police. Since he did not choose any such non-lethal alternative, she ruled he had committed culpable homicide (manslaughter), a lesser crime than murder. She sentenced him to five years in prison.

Engrossed by this 'trial of the century,' the world reacted instantly to this judgement. In Glasgow, many lambasted Strathclyde University for not immediately rescinding Oscar's honorary doctorate. Four months later, that institution of higher learning complied. Susan Jack of the domestic abuse charity, Glasgow Women's Aid, spoke for many of the Blade Runner's critics: "I'm delighted the university has finally acted. He is not an appropriate role model." History was being rewritten in hopes of erasing his image from public consciousness. If his name came up, people would increasingly ask, as my neighbor recently did, "Who is Oscar Pistorius?"

However

Besides her meticulous weighing of all available evidence, what stands out most in Judge Masipa's lengthy decision was her emphasis that:

> "The deceased was killed under very peculiar circumstances. There are indeed a number of aspects in the case that do not make sense, such as:
>
> • Why the accused did not ascertain from the deceased when he heard the window open, whether she too had heard anything.
>
> • Why he did not ascertain whether the deceased had heard him since he did not get a response from the deceased before making his way to the bathroom.

- Why the deceased was in the toilet and only a few metres away from the accused, did not communicate with the accused, or phone the police as requested by the accused. This the deceased could have done, irrespective of whether she was in the bedroom or in the toilet, as she had her cell phone with her. It makes no sense to say she did not hear him scream, 'get out'. It was the accused version that he screamed on top of his voice, when ordering the intruders to get out.

- Why the accused fired not one, one shot but four shots, before he ran back to the bedroom to try to find the deceased."

Judge Masipa chose to not conjecture about possible meanings of these and other highly significant, incomprehensible aspects of Oscar's testimony. Instead, she pronounced her verdict and the reasoning behind it.

Earlier, Bail Magistrate Desmond Nair had highlighted similar matters in Oscar's account that made absolutely no sense to the magistrate. After months of detailed evidence, testimony, and rigorous cross-examination, the literally gut-wrenching trial terminated with no light whatsoever being shed on any of these extremely important points. (Oscar was so overwhelmed as he relived the tragedy during the trial that he was provided a green plastic bucket into which he could vomit.) These many mysterious issues continued to completely defy comprehension. Fortunately, having grasped the significance of these essential enigmas, both Bail Magistrate Nair and Judge Masipa included them prominently in their pronouncements. They stood out conspicuously for all to see, ponder, or ignore.

Most people paid little or no heed to these enormous anomalies. What simply registered with them was that Oscar had been found not guilty of murder, but guilty of homicide.

It behoves those who are seriously concerned with crime and justice to carefully attend to and probe more deeply into these baffling enigmas.

If we do not just glance over these astounding lacunae in Oscar's otherwise coherent, credible narrative, what difference might that make? If we allow these anomalies to register with full force, stimulating our reflective capacities, what on earth might we make of them? I propose that these puzzling points provide the crucial keys for comprehending this otherwise incomprehensible crime. Unless we understand the profoundly bewildering, central aspects of this case that Bail Magistrate Nair and Judge Masipa highlighted, this crime and trial, and Reeva's death, make no sense. Exploring and explaining these enigmas, this book will serve as amicus curiae (friend of the court), an 'expert witness' to the mother of all courts, the Court of Public Opinion.

Before I suggest how it is possible to make extremely valuable sense and use of these deep mysteries that permeate the Blade Runner's testimony, let us first turn our attention to and examine another strikingly odd, highly informative, legal case. This other tragedy and trial are extremely interesting and thought provoking in their own right. Beyond that, this other case will provide necessary contextual elements that will set the stage for our detailed analysis of Oscar's situation. While these two peculiar cases are by no means identical, there are useful similarities pertaining to certain underlying principles. These connections will prove very helpful to us in our efforts to unravel the glaring enigmas in the Blade Runner's tragic case.

PART II

Essential Background Concepts

Chapter 4

MAYHEM IN DURHAM

Kenneth James Parks and his high school sweetheart, Karen, had a beautiful five-month-old daughter, Melissa. Ken began suffering from severe insomnia and anxiety related to a gambling compulsion he developed in hopes of financing a surprise trip for his wife to visit her native land, Australia. Despite having lost much money betting on horseraces, he believed his initial win indicated a gift for picking winners. Soon his sad fortunes would reverse, he was sure. He just had to persevere.

Increasingly desperate for acquiring the means to finance his risky hobby, Kenneth created fraudulent invoices at work. Unlike his gambling, this activity brought him tens of thousands of dollars , enabling him to continue his passionate pursuit.

When Kenneth's embezzlement was discovered in March 1987, he was fired and court proceedings were initiated against him. To repay his employer, Karen and Ken put their home up for sale. Succumbing to his wife's urging, Ken attended Gamblers Anonymous. With further pressure from Karen, he made a commitment that on Saturday, May 23, he would tell his grandmothers—one of whom he had lived with during his high school years—about his gambling problems, the court proceedings, his unemployment, and their financial woes. The next day, Sunday, he would tell Karen's parents the same things at a family barbeque at his in-laws' home.

On the Thursday before that heavy confessional weekend, Karen discovered Ken had forged several checks in her name and had resumed gambling. Disappointed and enraged, she banished him from the marital bed. A few days later, Ken reneged on his promise to acknowledge his wrongdoings and their ramifications to his grandmothers. Instead, he opted to play rugby.

The following day, around 1:30 a.m., just hours before his scheduled confession with his in-laws, Ken dozed off on the living room couch while watching *Saturday Night Live*. That particular episode of the popular television show contained several violent scenes. Not long after falling asleep, Kenneth got out of bed and drove fourteen miles (10 to 15 minutes) from his home in Pickering, a small city just east of Toronto in the Regional Municipality of Durham, to his wife's parents' home in the Toronto suburb, Scarborough. Carrying a tire iron from his automobile, he proceeded to their bedroom. He stabbed and choked his father-in-law into unconsciousness and assaulted his mother-in-law repeatedly with a kitchen knife, then beat her to death with the tire iron.

When this emotional tornado subsided, Kenneth drove to the police station. Covered in blood, shaking in distress, he declared: "I just killed someone with my bare hands; oh my God ...I've just killed my mother- and father-in-law. I stabbed and beat them to death."

Ken told the police he could not recall anything after having fallen asleep until the moment he found himself looking down at his mother-in-law's sad face. Her mouth and eyes were open. She had a "frightened 'help-me' look." Hearing screams from his wife's younger siblings who slept upstairs, he ran to them shouting, "Kids, kids, kids." He wanted to reassure them. For a few moments, he stood outside the door behind which they cowered, then he left. Later, they said they never heard him shouting. They did recall him making grunting "animal noises" like people sometimes utter in their sleep.

In terms of the logical quality of Kenneth's narrative, what reassurance could those children possibly get from the man they used to love who had just brutally assaulted their parents? Despite the absurdity of his statement that he wanted to reassure them, perhaps it was true at some level of psychic reality. He may have wanted to inform them that he had no intention of harming them and that there was no one else in their home who would endanger them.

When Kenneth became fully aware of the catastrophe in which he had participated, he concocted wild explanations that exonerated him from culpability. He was sure someone must have drugged him, hauled him to his car, then drove him to his in-laws' home. There, he must have started to revive. In that semi-conscious state, he imagined he must have realized that the malevolent stranger who brought him there was now trying to murder his mother-in-law. Struggling to protect her from this vicious assailant, Ken's hands were badly cut.

Kenneth admitted there were problems with this scenario that he had constructed. What stranger would have wanted to do all that? How did that person get into Ken's house to drug the Kool-Aid Ken had consumed that evening? How could they have carried this tall, three hundred ten pound man to his car, and why would they? Although this tale was farfetched, to Kenneth it seemed no more bizarre than the alternative idea that featured him not being able to remember having driven fourteen miles prior to entering his in-laws' home, then violently attacking relatives he loved. Even after his preliminary trial, he continued to be convinced that his imaginative explanation was correct. The evidence, particularly his distraught confusion at the police station, all pointed that way, he told himself and others.

Kenneth's defense attorney, Marlys Edwardh, worked with other prominent lawyers in an elegant brownstone directly across the leafy, tree-lined street from where I practiced as a clinical psychologist and psychoanalyst. Marlys is married to a well-known forensic psychologist, Graham Turrall. Graham worked several meters down the hall from me. To begin making sense of the strange details of this case, Marlys and Graham, together with other professionals, considered an astonishing hypothesis. Was it possible that Kenneth may have committed this shocking crime while sleepwalking?

Chapter 5

THE (RELATIVELY) NEW SCIENCE OF SLEEP

The modern era of research into sleep and its anomalies was inaugurated in the mid Twentieth Century at the University of Chicago. There in the 1950s, physiologist Nathaniel Kleitman developed a method for investigating what happens in our crania and the rest of our bodies during sleep. Electrodes he attached to subjects' heads recorded brain waves and eye movements.

Sleep, Professor Kleitman discovered, is divided into approximately ninety-minute cycles. In the first stage, major physiological systems quiet down, as if we are entering hibernation. Respiration and heart rate decrease; body temperature drops; brain waves shift from the rapid, waking rate to high-amplitude, slow waves. After about 90 minutes, bodily systems begin to revive, except for major muscles that relax abruptly, as the eyes start moving quickly behind closed lids. During this *active* or *rapid eye movement (REM) sleep*, if one awakens subjects, they usually report dreams. (REM sleep and its relation to dreaming had been noted in 1937 by another University of Chicago physiologist, Edward Jacobson). If you arouse subjects during non-REM periods, they are less likely to report dreams. They may report a thought or a simple dream image. These NREM dreams typically lack the narrative complexity and weird features we associate with more shareworthy dreams.

There are exceptions to every rule. Some people, such as light sleepers, do have more complex dreams during NREM sleep. These individuals are sometimes referred to as *nonREM dreamers*. People in highly anxious states and individuals deprived of REM sleep are also prone to these more complex NREM dreams. They occur more toward the end of a night's sleep rather than in the beginning.

Nathaniel Kleitman's research led to a deluge of studies with human volunteers and animals. Soon his techniques were applied to troubled sleepers. A new medical subspecialty was born. In 1968, Canadian neurologist and neuroscientist Roger Broughton became the Director of possibly the world's first Sleep Medicine Center. Similar clinics, treating a growing variety of nocturnal problems, opened at other university-affiliated facilities. In 1975, the American Academy of Sleep Medicine was founded. Their International Classification of Sleep Disorders has undergone several revisions. Over seventy-five different sleep disorders have been identified. This number continues to expand.

New technologies, such as positron emission tomography (PET) scans and functional magnetic resonance imaging (fMRI), provide ever more sophisticated ways of observing what goes on in our brains. These machines enabled us to see that there are different patterns of activation and deactivation in the brain during the three states we cycle through every twenty-four hours (waking, NREM and REM sleep). During REM, there is less activity in the prefrontal cortex, the seat of our executive functions (logical thinking, judgment, decision-making, self-reflection). There is increased activity in sensory association areas and sites associated with emotion (limbic and paralimbic regions). In healthy people, the level of heightened activation in these regions is greater than that manifested while awake. The implication is that during REM sleep we are likely to see and hear illogical things that have emotional associations. Unhealthy subjects, such as those suffering from major depression or sleepwalking, may have different patterns of activation and deactivation in these brain areas.

Somnambulism

Following his pioneering laboratory research demonstrating that sleepwalking typically begins following an EEG (electroencephalographic) awakening reaction during slow brain wave nonREM sleep, Broughton (Gastaut & Broughton, 1965; Broughton, 1968) proceeded to define not only somnambulism but also nocturnal terrors and confusional awakenings as nonREM *disorders of arousal*.

Commenting on the Kenneth Parks case, Berit Brogaard (2012), Director of University of Miami's Brogaard Lab for Multisensory Research, and Kristian Marlow noted that normally sleepers are not consciously aware of sensory input from their surroundings. Furthermore, a gating mechanism blocks input from their cognitive brain to their motor system. The chemical messenger gamma-aminobutyric acid (GABA) inhibits the brain's motor system. In less contemporary neurophysiological terms, Sigmund Freud, the Viennese neurologist who went on to found psychoanalysis as a subdiscipline of psychology, wrote that it is safe for us to indulge forbidden impulses while dreaming because *access to motility* has been disabled. In somnambulism, this important gating mechanism is defective, allowing the brain to issue effective commands to our muscles.

In children, neurons that release GABA are still developing. They have not yet fully established a network of connections to keep motor activity under control. Consequently, many youngsters occasionally sleepwalk. As they get older, they usually no longer engage in these nocturnal strolls. For some adults, this gating mechanism remains underdeveloped, or functions less effectively due to sleep deprivation, fever, anxiety, or drugs. As a result, they continue having somnambulistic episodes.

In terms of these risk factors that can weaken this important gating mechanism, Kenneth Parks, immediately prior to his brutal actions, was very anxious about his radically changed life circumstances and he was suffering from severe insomnia. If, additionally, he had any of the neurophysiological vulnerabilities that facilitate somnambulism, he would have been a very strong candidate for nocturnal rambling.

In addition to the slow delta brain waves that occur during sleepwalking, there are significant amounts of high oscillation waves, like those that occur in fully awake people. Sleepwalkers are essentially *awake and asleep simultaneously*. They have their eyes open and can see, but not consciously. Areas of the brain that correlate with awareness, cognition, and voluntary movement remain asleep. Their actions are controlled by other parts of the brain and are more or less reflexive.

Some people not only walk and talk while asleep but also perform more complicated actions. Brogaard & Marlow cited several intriguing cases. Former chef Rob Wood cooked spaghetti bolognaise and fish and chips while asleep. An Australian woman regularly got out of bed at night and engaged in sex with strangers. 36-year-old Welsh-Australian artist, Lee Hadwin, has been getting up in his sleep since he was fourteen. Only the following morning does he discover that he has produced surrealistic and fantastical art. Typically he does not recall having created these works. He does frequently have vivid dreams of painting but has no interest in, or ability to paint during the daytime. Lee has had requests for his productions from galleries and museums. Now he goes by the name Kipasso, a moniker that sounds like the famous artist, Picasso, and *Que Paso*, Spanish for the obviously highly relevant question, "What's happening?" Clearly very complicated action sequences can take place while we are in states of *paradoxical sleep* in which we are essentially unconscious and asleep but nonetheless behave in many ways like individuals who are conscious and awake.

Chapter 6

SOMNAMBULISTIC KILLING

With the hypothesis of sleepwalking in mind, some puzzling details in Kenneth Parks' case began to make sense. Consider renowned sleep specialist Carlos Schenck's (2007) report of how one of his patients described the manner in which his *sleep terrors* morphed over the years. When single and living by himself, his nocturnal terror behavior focused around attempts to protect himself from imagined dangers. He would barricade himself in a room, or run to escape. After he married and had children, these activities shifted to protecting his family. He would frantically defend his wife from imagined intruders, then go to safeguard the children. His caring intent accords with Kenneth Parks' theory that he had been trying to save his in-laws by fighting off their attacker, before charging upstairs to assist their terrified children. Likewise, Oscar Pistorius repeatedly stated he was simply trying to defend himself and Reeva against the serious harm home invaders would otherwise have inflicted on them.

Despite Kenneth Parks having cut several of his fingers to the bone, severing tendons and nerves, when he arrived at the police station, he did not appear to be in pain. Police officers took him to Toronto's Sunnybrook Hospital's emergency room to have his injuries treated. This lack of pain is familiar to sleep specialists who refer to it as *somnambulistic dissociative analgesia*.

Prior to trial, Ken underwent rigorous laboratory sleep investigation, psychiatric interviews, and psychological tests. Electroencephalographic (EEG) scans revealed abnormal brain activity during deep sleep, combined with periods of partial awakenings, a pattern indicative of *parasomnia*. (Para means beyond, near, beside, sometimes implying an alteration or modification; somnia means sleep.) After careful examination of this data and all other evidence, five North American sleep experts could find no plausible explanation for Kenneth's crime other than somnambulism. One of those specialists, Dr. Roger Broughton, did not initially believe this complex series of actions could have been accomplished during sleep. After thorough investigation, he concurred that somnambulism was, indeed, the most likely explanation.

These specialists described Kenneth's actions as the result of many circumstances converging: he had plans to fix his in-laws' furnace; he was familiar with the route he would take to get to their home; he was restless from anxiety and worried about his upcoming trial. They postulated that it had suddenly occurred to Ken in his sleep that he should fix his in-law's furnace. Thoughts or dreams during non-REM sleep often concern relatively mundane matters. Unlike in healthy, normal sleep, access to his motor system was not disconnected. He was therefore able to get out of bed and drive to their abode. Inside their home, he was startled, perhaps by their attempts to awaken him. Without knowing what he was doing, he attacked his beloved in-laws.

The sleep specialists' theory concerning these motives for Ken's horrific assault accords with findings from a study published by Dr. Mark Pressman in 2007 in the respected professional journal, *Sleep*. Somnambulists are rarely violent and do not seek out victims while they are in a sleep arousal state. If a sleepwalker does become violent, the victim is usually someone who just got in the way, rather than being the target of premeditated violence, Pressman concluded after reviewing medical and legal literature on 32 cases. He sought to test the hypothesis that sleepwalkers may harm people who touch them or are close by, but they do not spontaneously attack other people. He divided the cases into three categories: sleepwalking; confusional arousal (a state identical to sleepwalking but the sleeper doesn't leave the bed); and sleep terrors, or sudden partial awakening due to a frightening stimulus, followed by sleepwalking. In all the confusional arousal cases, the victim of violence had been close to or touching the attacker, he found, and the same was true in 81 percent of sleep terror cases, and 40 to 90 percent of the sleepwalking cases. Often the provocation was quite minor and the response greatly exaggerated. The absence of detailed clinical histories for the defendants in the sleepwalking cases as well as the absence of transcripts of expert testimony or reports submitted by the experts made it impossible to determine which defendants were bona fide somnambulists who were likely to have been sleepwalking during the violent criminal act. Thus, in the absence of other data and evidence, the presence of proximity and/or provocation could only be said to range from 40% to 90% in that group.

In learning from Pressman's research, we should keep in mind that although up to 90% of violent sleepwalking may be provoked by people confronting sleepwalkers, rather than sleepwalkers seeking confrontations, a significant 10% to 60% of violent somnambulistic incidents may not be provoked by people confronting sleepwalkers. Further research would be helpful.

Somnambulism does not automatically lead to full acquittal, Brogaard & Marlow, the scientists mentioned earlier, noted. If an involuntary act originated in a disease of the mind, the accused might be judged not guilty by reason of insanity and confined to a psychiatric facility until it is established that he is no longer dangerous. A condition stemming from the psychological makeup of the accused, rather than external factors, could lead to a verdict of at least temporary insanity. Either of these two conditions might justify less than full acquittal of sleepwalkers who kill.

The defense team at Kenneth Parks' trial argued that the tragic killing was caused by a combination of severe external factors: loss of employment; marital stress; upcoming confessions to relatives; necessity to put their home up for sale; and his imminent trial. As it was unlikely that a similar clustering of so many stressful variables would ever occur again, further incidents of aggressive sleepwalking by Ken were extremely unlikely, they concluded. Supporting this position is the 1995 report by Guilleminault et alia – written several years after Kenneth Parks' trial—that presented the fortunate, though unexplained finding that such sleep-related violence seldom recurs.

The prosecution had their own sleep experts attending Kenneth's historic legal proceedings. They did not challenge the defense's expert witnesses. The Court also accepted the defense position. The verdict was that this tragedy was a case of homicide during *non-insane automatism*, part of a presumed somnambulistic episode. Ken did not have any preexisting disease of the mind within the meaning of the Criminal Code. There was no evidence of psychosis or other mental pathology. Accordingly, he was a free man—though hardly free from whatever guilt, shame, and other heavy feelings and consequences he may have carried with him as he exited that courtroom.

Disagreeing with this surprising verdict, the State appealed the Court's decision all the way to the Supreme Court. At each step in this process, every court upheld the initial acquittal. Not surprisingly, this unusual, terrible story made headlines around the world.

Anticipating likely widespread skepticism about this verdict, the Supreme Court felt the need to address this matter:

It may be that some will regard the exoneration of an accused through a defence of somnambulism as an impairment of the credibility of our justice system. Those who hold this view would also reject insane automatism as an excuse from criminal responsibility. However, these views are contrary to certain fundamental precepts of our criminal law: only those who act voluntarily with the requisite intent should be punished by criminal sanction.

A full-length, reader friendly account of this unsettling story is available in renowned journalist and author June Callwood's 1990 book, *The Sleepwalker*. Kenneth Parks' highly compelling narrative also became the basis for a made-for-television movie. Thorough discussion of this case by the sleep experts and forensic psychologist who participated in the trial can be found in Broughton et alia's 1994 article in *Sleep*.

In their post-trial reflections, Broughton et al. stated that the main conditions in which sleep related violence occurs are during: abrupt *confusional arousal* from sleep; somnambulism; and *rapid eye movement (REM) sleep behavior disorder (RBD)*. Attempted and completed sleep-related homicides are not new, they noted. Documented cases go back to the Middle Ages. In one instance, a somnambulistic man strangled his wife and struck her head with an ax. Fortunately she lived and testified to her "perfect husband's" virtues. In Kenneth Parks' case, Karen likewise stood steadfastly by her man throughout the legal process, even though her family was perturbed by her loyalty.

Reflecting on Kenneth's case after the trial, the defense team's experts remained convinced that his homicidal violence had almost certainly occurred during somnambulism. However, two major issues were still obscure, they wrote. First, why did he go to his parents-in-law's residence? In court it was suggested that he had in mind his promise to do some household repairs for them. The tire iron would have been a tool he could use in that project. Even more compelling to me than that explanation is the specialists' subsequent belief that Ken's planned visit to confess his severe difficulties to his in-laws the very next day was a major stressful event that would have been on his mind when he fell asleep. This latter idea accords better with Freud's assertion that one can always find a "day residue" that triggers a dream. Ken's imminent, humiliating confession provided a powerful trigger. The home repairs were, in contrast, a less pressing matter.

The second obscure issue that concerned the experts was why the aggression occurred. As mentioned earlier, they suspected Ken's in-laws discovered him wandering around their residence and interfered with his behavior, precipitating his extreme response. It is generally difficult to deflect sleepwalkers from ongoing behaviors that appear preprogrammed. It is as if the behavioral sequence has to run itself out, they noted.

A less benign hypothesis that I would be inclined to favor would be that Kenneth may not have just been wandering about his in-law's residence kindly contemplating an altruistic, thoughtful home repair project. Rather, he may have arrived there during a state of somnambulistic dream enactment—armed and ready to kill. This phenomenon, known as *dreamwalking*—non-REM dreaming combined with somnambulism—will be explored in the next chapter.

Chapter 7

THE STUFF OF WHICH DREAMS AND DERANGEMENT ARE MADE

On the day preceding Kenneth Parks' somnambulistic (dreamwalking) episode, he found it necessary to at least procrastinate on his painful promise to tell his grandmothers about the serious difficulties into which he had gotten himself. Karen was furious that he avoided these first two rounds of family confession. He was now under enormous pressure to make three separate confessions the next day. One can understand that he might have anticipated sunrise as the dawn of a bloody Sunday.

Steeling himself for these confessions, Brogaard & Marlow believed Ken felt ashamed and feared abandonment, especially by his wife and her family. I imagine he might well have felt he would *die of shame*, perhaps many times, during that upcoming, grueling, confessional marathon. In such circumstances, his unconscious, desperate, defensive, Darwinian, dreaming mind might have felt, as some survival-oriented minds are inclined to reason: Instead of me being terrorized to death on Sunday, let it be the other party who suffers that bloody fate. In panicky states of mind, it can seem as if the only two options are kill or be killed. With this impulse toward self-preservation, Ken's parasomnia may have commenced.

In a similar style of reasoning, Ken had felt earlier that he must embezzle funds to continue gambling in a frantic, escalating effort to at least recoup what he had lost lest he have to humiliatingly admit that he had squandered the family's finances, in which case he would surely perish from shame in front of his wife, his relatives, friends, and acquaintances. To dodge that dire fate, he may have felt he had no choice but to take criminal actions, even if they could (and did) have disastrous consequences.

To escape his primitive terror of being overwhelmed, abandoned, humiliated, and psychically annihilated by his imminent Sunday admissions, Kenneth's dreaming self may have been moved rapidly to project his feared, concretized, terminal fate onto his in-laws. This defensive tour de force would serve to omnipotently counteract his otherwise inevitable demise. As a result of this psychic dark magic, Ken could now feel: I am not helpless, impotent, about to be clobbered, abandoned, humiliated, ruined, devastated and destroyed. On the contrary, I am safe, extremely potent, invulnerable. It is others who are unprotected, endangered, helpless, terrified, and destined to be obliterated. This self-protective reversal—forcefully extruding one's helpless terror into others—is sometimes known as the defense mechanism of projective identification (or, one might say, projective disidentification).

Shame

Can shame and the related fear of excommunication and abandonment really drive people to kill? Lest anyone doubt the power of such sentiments to propel murderous impulses, consider Associated Press journalist Kathy Gannon's recent report from Pakistan. She described a young woman, Zeenat, marrying someone whom her family did not approve. Zeenat's mother, Parveen Rafiq, and her uncle lured her back home, promising to prepare her appropriately for a proper wedding. Instead of honoring that commitment, Rafiq felt it was more appropriate to strangle her unsuspecting offspring until she was nearly dead. She proceeded to douse her daughter with kerosene, then set her on fire.

Seeing smoke emerging from Raffiq's tiny apartment, neighbors rushed to the scene. They heard Rafiq hollering from the rooftop: "I have killed my daughter. I have saved my honor. She will never shame me again." The women outside all sided with Rafiq. Even after her arrest, they continued their support. All agreed she should be released. "It's better to have no children than to have a daughter who brings you shame," one opined. In a pedagogical spirit, she added: "This is a good lesson for all the girls here to protect the family honor, to not bring disrespect."

In another case in that same nation, a mother slit the throat of her pregnant daughter whom, she believed, brought similar shame to her family by marrying the man she loved. If someone is to die of humiliation, tradition demands it be the one who dared follow her heart, not the other family members experiencing the shame to which their group subscribes. Death before dishonor.

In yet another instance, this time in the city of Abbotabad, a teenage girl was tortured, injected with poison, then strapped to the seat of a vehicle that was then parked outside a bus stop, doused with gasoline and set ablaze. The resulting conflagration broadcast a powerful message to the community. What, you may ask, had been this adolescent's horrific crime that merited such consequences? She had helped a friend to elope. Her execution was ordered by the local council of elders. Those wise men dictated the precise manner in which her death sentence should be carried out.

Similar gruesome reports abound. Ms. Gannon noted that three people *per day* were killed in Pakistan in 2016 for bringing shame to their families. This grim statistic represented an increase of ten per cent over the previous year. These appalling figures are just the known instances. There are many more unreported 'honor killings'. The perpetrators of these retaliatory crimes are rarely punished because sharia law allows killers' families to forgive those who have carried them out.

It is not just in Pakistan and nearby countries that shame murders are perpetrated. Historians tell us that one of the major factors leading to the rise of the German Nazis was the humiliation that nation experienced under the terms imposed by the Allies when Deutschland lost the First World War. It is not just individuals, but subcultures and nations states that can be driven by blind fury, fueled by shame, to annihilate others who are deemed to be the source, or at least good scapegoats, for their embarrassment.

Scratching the Itch to Kill

Sigmund Freud is widely recognized as one of the most brilliant, controversial minds in intellectual history. Shortly after the outbreak of World War One, in an article entitled *Thoughts for the Times on War and Death,* he shared his belief that we are all at least unconsciously similar to murderers (like those Pakistani women and German Nazis). This is not a pleasant thought, but it is one that makes sense, unless we want to soothe ourselves with the belief that those people and subcultures are simply alien monstrosities that in no way resemble who we are or could become, even in our wildest, darkest dreams.

Reflecting on the barbarism that was so common during the First World War, Freud stated that the widespread disillusionment with respect to these supposedly highly evolved societies was not entirely justified. People's disenchantment arose from the shattering of the illusion that we had become far more international and civilized than was actually the case, he believed. We can console ourselves that our painful disappointment with respect to modern savagery is unjustified, he wrote. It was our expectations, based on illusion, that were unwarranted. Citizens had not sunk so low as we feared because they had never risen so high as we had imagined. Freud concluded his *Thoughts for the Times* with a plea that we temper, or replace, our naïve illusions about the human mind with a greater appreciation of the psyche's true nature.

Of what does this psychic actuality that Freud believes we should embrace, rather than deny, consist? It begins with what he refers to as the primal and continuing *ambivalence of feeling* we have toward people. Commencing in infancy with our mothers, we experience intense love and hate. During acculturation, two factors—one internal, the other external—are brought to bear on our hateful impulses. The external variable pertains to the pressure exercised by upbringing—the many claims of our cultural environment. The internal factor is exercised by the human need for love that transforms egoistic instincts into social ones. We learn to value being loved as an advantage for which we are willing to sacrifice other pursuits.

Civilization of individuals and societies is attained through these twin pressures to renounce aggressive and other instinctual gratifications. In this lengthy, arduous process, primitive hateful impulses meet many fates. They are inhibited; directed toward other aims and fields; turned back on the self; become comingled with other impulses; and/or alter their objects. For example, murderous rage at a parent may be *defensively displaced* onto a cat, frog, or insect. Under the aegis of *reaction formation*, another of the many intrapsychic defenses brought to bear on hostile impulses, unacceptable cruelty appears to be transformed into valued caring.

The environment not only offers love benefits but also utilizes other rewards and punishments to motivate us to surrender or suppress violent urges, Freud noted. Under the influence of such incentives, a person may choose to behave well, even though no genuine transformation of egoism into altruism has occurred. This superficial behavior modification only holds as long as it is advantageous.

Freud's intriguing research convinced him that every earlier stage (e.g., primitive hate) persists alongside later stages that have arisen from it. In this model of development, succession involves co-existence. "The earlier mental state may not have manifested itself for years, but none the less it is so far present that it may at any time again become the mode of expression of the forces of the mind, and indeed the only one, as though all later developments had been annulled or undone. ...The primitive mind is, in the fullest meaning of the word, imperishable" (p. 285).

A corollary to this view of psychic progression and structure formation concerns the perpetual readiness and desire of inhibited instincts to break through into consciousness and action. Repressed impulses seek satisfaction at any possible opportunity—an outcome famously described by Freud as *the return of the repressed.* Contemporary psychoanalysts often speak more of dissociated self-states or disavowed relational configurations rather than repudiated impulses. Regardless of terminology, all are endeavoring to comprehend the same problematic phenomena that concerned Freud.

Nations may recapitulate this course of individual development, including the unstable status quo it achieves, Freud suggested. Despite countries' remarkable accomplishments, capacity for regression to primitive, less libidinally unified states is preserved. Hateful, destructive impulses remain alive, available to burst forth and wreak havoc. With a pinch of cynicism, Freud remarked that: "The state has forbidden the individual the practice of wrongdoing, not because it desires to abolish it, but because it desires to monopolize it, like salt and tobacco" (p. 279). Belligerent nations permit themselves every possible violent misdeed, every lie and deception that would disgrace any individual committing such acts, he observed.

Contemplating the dead bodies of their loved ones, Freud postulated that our ancestors were moved to begin developing: new beliefs in the immortality of the soul; a sense of guilt; and the earliest ethical commandments. The first and most important of those prohibitions was: "Thou shalt not kill." This primal taboo was, he believed, acquired out of our ambivalence toward deceased loved ones. It was a reaction against the satisfaction of the hatred for them hidden behind grief. This commandment was gradually extended to strangers who were not loved and, ultimately, even to enemies.

Such a powerful ethical prohibition can only arise from, and be directed against an equally powerful, opposite inclination, Freud averred. This first commandment "makes it certain that we spring from an endless series of generations of murderers, who had the lust for killing in their blood, as, perhaps, we ourselves have today" (p. 296). The history of the world that our children learn at school is essentially a series of murders of peoples, he noted. "If we are to be judged by our unconscious wishful impulses, we ourselves are, like primeval man, a gang of murderers," Freud bluntly wrote. In the unconscious, "We daily and hourly get rid of anyone who stands in our way, of anyone who has offended or injured us. ...Our unconscious will murder even for trifles; like the ancient Athenian code of Draco, it knows no other punishment for crime than death" (p. 297). More than we might like to think, we are all cut from rather similar cloth as are those Pakistani women, German Nazis, and other killers.

Durham Derailment

Prior to Kenneth's wife leaving their home for work, just hours before the violent crime, they had their worst ever argument. She informed her spouse that as soon as their house sold, she would leave him and take their daughter with her. Later she softened that threat. Only if Ken failed to straighten up would she and Melissa leave.

When one examines the many cases where men have murdered their wives and girlfriends, one finds with monotonous regularity that the women had been considering, or actually planning, to part. For these vulnerable men, this threat of abandonment triggers terror, rage, shame, and regressive, pathological functioning. Despite their often considerable accomplishments in other spheres of living, they are, as Freud said, not nearly as civilized as people who knew them typically believed. So often their neighbors and friends tell investigators that these killers had just seemed to be normal, even pleasant, members of the community—like us.

One can imagine Kenneth struggling with similarly intense feelings and murderous counter-reactions, perhaps just unconsciously, in relation to his wife's threat to abandon him. Dreaming is one realm in which such phantasies can safely manifest, often in highly disguised forms. That sleeping state can provide a safety valve for expressing otherwise unacceptable sentiments. We often acknowledge this fact with the aphorism that mad men do what sane ones merely dream.

Kenneth's defense team asserted that he had no motive for killing his in-laws. Au contraire, he liked his wife's family very much. Things can, however, play out very differently in the unconscious from which Ken's violence arose. In that realm, powerful motives like shame, anger, and fear of abandonment may have gone into overdrive. In that underground domain, to protect his primary love object, Karen, who was pressuring him to make these painful confessions, Ken might have unconsciously *displaced* murderous impulses toward her onto her parents. Displacement is a key feature of the *primary process cognition* characteristic of the unconscious.

When the police went to Ken and Karen's home, they anticipated finding Karen and baby Melissa dead. Based on their experience, they expected that Ken's murderous rage would have included his wife rather than being entirely discharged onto his in-laws. Blessedly, they found both Karen and Melissa alive and well.

At the hospital where his slashed hand was being

treated, Kenneth not only believed *both* his in-laws might be dead, but also wondered if he might have 'hurt' Karen. Unsure of the extent of mayhem he had perpetrated, he would not have been surprised if she had been among his victims (perhaps even the prime target). In a complementary vein, Karen wept: "I wish it had been me instead. Why couldn't it have been me he killed? ...It's my fault." Continuing to blame herself, she added, "I should have known what he was going to do. I should have known what kind of a mood he was in." Her regret is what is sometimes called survivor guilt.

In addition to fearing imminent mortification and fatal excommunication by his wife and extended family for all his crimes and misdemeanors, Kenneth's dread of abandonment may have had other sources. Lady Luck had already abandoned him at the racetrack. Likewise, his employer had tossed him out. Furthermore, it is not uncommon for men to experience abandonment anxiety and anger when their wives turn their attention to newborns. These mothers are often not only in love with their offspring but also exhausted by pregnancy, parturition, and subsequent sleep deprivation. In that postpartum context, Ken's original enchantment with his baby daughter disappeared after a few weeks. He took little interest in her. He refused to diaper or bathe her, or get up at night when she cried. When asked to hold her, he would not. There were, therefore, indications that he may have already been feeling emotionally abandoned by Karen's natural preoccupation with Melissa, long before she actually threatened to move out and take their daughter with her. In this situation, Ken may have initiated a counter-abandonment process. It can feel far superior to defensively abandon others (such as Karen and Melissa), rather than feeling passively abandoned by them.

Kenneth's father, Jim, possessed (or was possessed by) a terrifying temper (like his somnambulistic son). He abandoned his wife and offspring when Ken was four years old. After the divorce, Jim cut off all communication with the family until Ken was eighteen. Kenneth never enjoyed a close relationship with his mother, either. If he had, that security might have compensated for the lack of intimate relationship with his father. When Ken's mother remarried, Ken developed a distant, somewhat difficult relationship with this stepfather.

In Kenneth's family, fear of abandonment, may have been built into his psyche long before he ever met Karen and her family due to his father's early desertion, perhaps compounded by whatever emotional limitations Ken's mother may have had, some of which may have been perceived by her offspring as emotional abandonment. The loving relationship he enjoyed with his parents-in-law helped to offset the lack of closeness with his biological parents. To lose this newfound love would be devastating. The possibility of such a loss would activate his psyche for emergency protective action.

When we are struggling with early abandonment trauma, we may unconsciously feel the only thing we can do to not feel like helpless victims is to *actively* perpetrate similar devastation on others, or even on ourselves. This manifestation of the *repetition compulsion,* Freud's insightful term, is sometimes referred to, in his daughter Anna's terminology, as the unconscious defense mechanism of *turning passive into active.* We seek to create at least the illusion of being masters of our destiny.

Fearing desertion by his wife and in-laws, Kenneth brought this very fate upon himself, as so often happens. Attempting unconsciously to reverse his dreaded destiny by actively 'abandoning' his daughter and then abandoning (eliminating) his in-laws, he ensured being 'abandoned' by them and their kin. Karen stood by him for quite some time after the crime. Ultimately, however, she did not feel she could continue to live with this person who had visited such violence on her parents. Kenneth brought about the very abandonment he so feared.

Chapter 8

DURHAM DISSENT

A writer is a world trapped in a person.
—Victor Hugo

After starting to gamble, Kenneth Parks stopped socializing and began to suffer from pressure headaches and insomnia, Brogaard & Marlow, the American scientists referred to earlier, noted. His weight increased from two hundred forty to three hundred ten pounds. Fired for embezzlement, his mental health deteriorated. He would wake up breathing heavily, feeling pressure on his chest. After consulting a doctor, he was treated for asthma. To Brogaard & Marlow, these symptoms suggested severe anxiety disorder related to underlying emotional problems for which he should have sought and received treatment.

They also thought Kenneth's social history supported their belief concerning his emotional problems. He had been a troubled child. He lacked close relationships with his parents and did not fare well in elementary school. In Junior High, he was arrested for petty theft. At age sixteen, his mother relocated to another community. Rather than separating from his familiar milieu, Ken moved in with his grandmother. Underlying emotional conflict related to these developmental stresses may have fueled his anxiety, uncontrollable gambling urges, theft, forgery, assaults and, ultimately, his killing spree.

Subtle, powerful, lingering effects of a troubled developmental history can be difficult to detect via some forms of psychiatric interviewing and psychological testing. From what we know about Kenneth's early history, there are grounds for thinking he might have had complications and problems in his foundational psychological architecture. Even for the brief time when his parents did live together, they struggled with marital challenges. Beginning life in the context of parental disharmony, stress, and preoccupation, Kenneth's *emotional* abandonment likely commenced far earlier than his parents' geographic separation and ultimate divorce.

Struggling with early physical and emotional abandonment and their ongoing sequellae, individuals may resort to various pathological defenses, such as *identification with the aggressor*. In this defensive process, one exits the victim role to become, instead, the powerful aggressor. Faced with the challenges of being a new parent, Ken seems to have psychologically abandoned his daughter and perhaps in some ways his wife, much as his father had done to Ken and Ken's mother years earlier. Instead of finding a way to become a pillar of support for his family, Kenneth focused on his own psychological needs, inadvertently robbing Karen and Melissa of needed emotional and financial resources.

Several details of Kenneth's situation were ignored during trial, Brogaard & Marlow believe. He was known for having some uncontrollable urges. Due to these peremptory impulses, he acquired a gambling debt, embezzled, forged checks, lost his job and home. His gambling misdeeds, with their huge financial and relational costs, caused him to suffer from extreme anxiety that, in turn, led to insomnia.

Kenneth used to have an excellent relationship with his in-laws, in part because when he first met their daughter, she was a runaway. He had convinced Karen to return home. Her parents continued to be grateful for this intervention. After being fired, Ken stopped visiting Karen's family. Unable to find full-time work, he did occasional jobs as an electrician. Hoping to supplement that income, he continued gambling. At the time of his vicious attacks, he was on bail, awaiting trial. Marital conflict had become severe. These factors, compounded by the acute stress generated by his multiple upcoming confessions, could have motivated him to drive twenty-three kilometers to slay Karen's parents in a fit of temporary insanity, Brogaard & Marlow believe.

Evidence collected prior to trial indicated some family and personal history of nocturnal ambulatory activity (parasomnia). Kenneth's grandfather used to walk around during his sleep, sometimes cooking food without eating it. One night, when Ken was eleven years old, his mother checked on him while he was supposedly just sleeping. Instead, Kenneth was headed out the sixth floor window. She grabbed him by the leg. This was the only instance of sleepwalking she could recall. Karen remembered Ken talking to her in his sleep and being a deep sleeper, difficult to awaken.

EEG readings during sleep tests Kenneth underwent were irregular, suggesting parasomnia, though Brogaard & Marlow say irregular readings can occur when people are under great stress (as Kenneth was) and abusing substances (which he was not). Was he really fully asleep the whole time, they wondered, or could he have been conscious, albeit temporarily insane, repressing the horrific memories almost immediately? They believe considerable evidence supports the latter hypothesis.

Sleepwalkers' brains process visual and auditory stimuli, but these sensory stimuli do not give rise to stable neuronal activity, Brogaard & Marlow note. Brain signals are not as strong as during waking states. Consequently, somnambulists normally can only complete tasks they have done hundreds of times before. To navigate safely, they must be in their usual surroundings. On vacation, they often bump into walls, stub toes, and harm themselves in other ways because their brains assume erroneously that they are in familiar surroundings.

Sleepwalking in his Mexico City hotel room, seventeen-year-old Canadian tennis player, Peter Polansky, broke a window, crawled out through the broken shards, and plummeted to the ground. Unlike Kenneth Parks, Polansky had no mother, or any other vigilant person to grab his leg and spare him that fall.

In some criminal cases it has been alleged that people who performed exceedingly complex actions in relatively unfamiliar surroundings and committed horrendous acts were sleepwalking. Equally complicated actions in relatively unfamiliar surroundings are unheard of in non-criminal cases, Brogaard & Marlow state. It is unlikely that enough visual information about the environment can be unconsciously processed for a person to be able to complete extremely complex maneuvers in relatively unfamiliar surroundings. Kenneth had not been to his in-laws' home since losing his job two months prior to the killing. In the dark of night, he would have had to drive unconsciously in somewhat unfamiliar surroundings, negotiating several major intersections. Ordinary drivers, when lost in thought, have at least some awareness, yet they miss exits or discover they have taken a route more familiar to them rather than one they had planned on following. They suddenly find themselves at their old home, their child's school, or their workplace, rather than at the venue to which they had intended to go. Brogaard & Marlow believe such considerations cast some doubt on the claim that Kenneth was fully asleep while he carried out his highly complex actions.

Sleepwalkers do not normally take long trips during their sleep. Kenneth's grandfather never left his home when sleepwalking. Though there were several people with parasomnia in the Parks family, few were sleepwalkers and only one, a second cousin, left the house during her nocturnal rambles. Although she made it outside, she simply sat there. No one in the family ever went on long trips while sleepwalking, or ended up carrying out highly complicated actions that appear to require conscious control.

It is also highly dubious, Brogaard & Marlow assert, that Kenneth could have stayed asleep during the whole violent ordeal. It is a myth that you cannot awaken a sleepwalker. It may be unwise to do so because they may then end up confused or terrified. But it is no harder to awaken a somnambulist than to awaken any other person in a state of deep sleep, they state.

Sleepwalkers' brains may unconsciously go into defense mode if startled, they acknowledge. Kenneth choked his father-in-law, beat up his mother-in-law with the tire iron, and stabbed both repeatedly with a kitchen knife. His mother-in-law sustained six stab wounds through her chest, one through her shoulder blade, and a fatal wound through her heart. These grotesque acts are not simply the result of a brain unconsciously going rogue after being startled, Brogaard & Marlow assert. The enormous, prolonged struggle by itself should have been enough to wake up a person in deep sleep, they state.

Police found Kenneth's in-laws' bed disheveled, the pillows soaked in blood. Their mattress had been moved around and the headboard was tipped forward. It seems, therefore, that he may have attacked them in their bed, rather than their having interfered with his intention of doing some household repairs in their basement. His murdered mother-in-law was discovered in a room five to six feet from their bedroom. It is implausible that such a severe struggle, with them screaming and pleading with him to back off, come to his senses, and spare their lives, would have failed to wake him up, Brogaard & Marlow claim.

When Kenneth arrived at the police station, severe cuts to his hands attested to his having been in a major struggle. The lack of pain he manifested can occur not only during sleepwalking, Brogaard & Marlow assert, but also in states of shock, great distress, and after drug use. The fact that Ken remembered his mother in-law's sad face with her eyes and mouth wide open as if pleading suggests his subsequent dissociative analgesia at the police station, which was a core piece of evidence in the trial, most likely was not due to being in a somnambulistic state, Brogaard & Marlow allege. They believe analgesia was more likely the result of his being in a state of shock or overwhelming distress. They also suggest his memory of his mother-in-law's sad face may have been a hallucination.

The evidence suggested to Brogaard & Marlow that Kenneth's actions were not entirely automatic. He must have been at least partially conscious but, owing to the gruesome nature of his actions, he may have repressed his memories of the details. They believe this hypothesis is consistent with other cases they have studied. For example, Paula Pinckard shot her eleven-year-old daughter, Aubrey, to death in their Rock Hill, Louisiana home in March 2000 prior shooting herself in the stomach in a suicide attempt during a Prozac-induced psychosis. Paula had to undergo hypnosis to remember any of these terrible events. Like Kenneth, she did not show any pain from her wounds when the paramedics arrived. The judge found her Not Guilty by Reason of Insanity. She was therefore committed to the custody of the State Department of Health and Hospital, Forensic Division.

People who are insane are considered incapable of intending to perform a criminal act because they either do not know the act is wrong or they cannot fully control their actions. Brogaard & Marlow find it plausible that, owing to temporary insanity, Kenneth Parks was not fully in control of his actions even if he was conscious of them. His actions would then be considered to have been voluntary but unintentional. "I just killed someone with my bare hands; oh my God," he exclaimed.

Reconciling Contradictions

After seeing his mother-in-law's sad face, Kenneth said he just sat there until he heard his wife's younger siblings screaming. He recalled thinking they were in trouble, needing help. "Kids, kids, kids," he claimed he yelled, as he went upstairs to reassure them. If he had really been sleepwalking when he was hollering those words at the children, he would not have been able to recall that moment so clearly afterwards, Brogaard & Marlow note. If, on the other hand, he were awake at the time, then he would not have made the grunting noises that were the only sounds the children heard him utter. He would have simply yelled, just as he remembered doing. Pointing out this contradiction, they are at least implicitly raising the possibility that he was both awake and asleep, either simultaneously or in an oscillating manner. This possibility would accord with subsequent electroencephalographic (EEG) scans of Ken's brain that showed abnormal neural activity during deep sleep combined with periods of partial awakenings.

Arguing that Kenneth had conscious control of his actions, Brogaard & Marlow cite Stephen Reitz' case. Stephen was having an affair with a woman whom he stabbed to death, allegedly while being asleep. District attorney Chris Frisco argued that in order to carry out relatively complex acts such as figuring out which end of the knife to hold and which end to use to stab a person, one has to have some conscious control of what one is doing. In Kenneth Parks' case, this line of reasoning could be used to support the opposite idea, namely that there were significant lacunae in his conscious control. Ken severed several hand tendons and nerves during his attack. He might not have fully known at all times which end of the knife to grasp. The harm he may have inflicted on himself further suggests he might have had oscillating degrees of awareness and conscious control, and lack of those attributes.

Although critical of the defense case that the Court accepted at Kenneth's trial, Brogaard & Marlow also raised a more integrative possibility. If sleepwalkers do not act as complete automatons, the question arises as to what extent they can be held responsible for their actions, even if they really are asleep while committing their crimes. If they have some conscious awareness during these events, and a motive, and cannot be acquitted on grounds of insanity, how much do their actions differ from those we all engage in? We might never have full autonomy. Sleepwalkers who commit crimes or produce artwork or culinary dishes may have some autonomy and hence only differ from people who are awake in degree rather than in kind. If so, then maybe full acquittal for crimes committed while people are asleep should never be an option, they suggest.

Kenneth Parks' case raises important questions not only about criminal responsibility and guilt but also about the relationships between sleeping, dreaming, and waking consciousness. All these issues that we will consider further in subsequent chapters are by no means simple, but they are interesting. We are coming to understand more about them all the time. There is still much more that we need to learn. Oscar Pistorius' case will assist us in this endeavor.

Post Acquittal

All the courts accepted the defense experts' opinion that Kenneth Parks was exceedingly unlikely to reoffend. At the time of the trial, I felt less confident about their prediction. They stated it was highly improbable Ken would ever encounter a similar set of stressful circumstances comparable to those that enabled the events at his in-laws' home. They recommended he avoid sleep deprivation and stress. Unfortunately, it is not uncommon for many individuals to face significant stress and sleep problems at various points in their lives. These risk factors are not always easy to avoid.

After release from his year of custody, Kenneth received psychotherapy to help him adjust to his new life. Hopefully that treatment may also have worked to resolve any prior underlying vulnerabilities in his personality—the stuff from which dreams, nightmares, and unconscious acting-out are made. Follow-up studies eighteen months after Ken's initial ones showed somewhat fragmented sleep but there was near total suppression of slow wave sleep (in which somnambulism occurs) due to the nightly medication he took (benzodiazepine oxazepam).

In 2006, the year Oscar Pistorius began studying for a Bachelor of Commerce degree at the University of Pretoria, Kenneth Parks' vocational interests also took a new turn. He ran for the position of school trustee in Durham. By then divorced, he now had six children. At least for nearly two decades, the sleep specialists proved correct in their belief that he would not re-offend. Many members of his community were, however, still not feeling very positively toward him. "I teach in education and my first concern would be a lack of ethics and lack of professionalism on somebody who is representing our school board," university professor Ann Lesage told television journalists at Toronto's *CityNews*. "Sleepwalking perhaps, a medical thing, but not the embezzlement," civil servant Alan MacDonald added.

From the Parks' tragedy and other killings I have mentioned, and still others I will discuss, we stand to learn a great deal that will be enormously helpful when we return to the main case study of this book, the recent tragedy of Reeva and Oscar.

Chapter 9

DREAMS AND PARASOMNIA

*The purpose of psychology is to give us
a completely different idea of the things
we know best. ...That which has always
been accepted by everyone, everywhere,
is almost certain to be false.*

—Paul Valéry, French poet,
in *Tel Quel* (1943)

I n another of his famously insightful statements, Sigmund Freud said that dreams are *the guardians of sleep.* The mysterious process of visually vivid, dramatic, nocturnal mentation has evolved via natural selection, partly in order to increase our chances of obtaining the restorative rest we need. Dreams attempt to manage stimulation that would otherwise awaken us. For example, Freud described someone's alarm clock ringing on a workday morning. Since they had had less sleep than they needed, they longed to stay in bed, rather than being ejected from it by that obnoxious alarm. Consequently, instead of realizing the clock had sounded, they dreamt that church bells were making beautiful sounds. These musical instruments were letting everyone know it was Sunday morning, time to rise for prayer. Since the sleeping individual was not planning on attending the church service, s/he did not have get up. The dream wrapped that annoying alarm in a much more harmonious, appealing narrative. The desire to continue sleeping was gratified. Such dreams also illustrate Freud's well-known assertion that *wish fulfillment* (in this case, the desire to sleep) is a central purpose of dreaming.

Much of the challenging stimulation with which dreams struggle to cope is not external, unlike the preceding alarm clock example, but arises from internal, psychological sources. After falling asleep, our minds continue grappling with challenging situations from our current lives. These stressful dilemmas are amplified by meanings those events have that derive from our complex personal histories (e.g., psychological conflicts and developmental microtraumata). Dreams, therefore, do battle on four fronts. They attempt to manage: ordinary external stimulation (like the alarm clock); common internal stimulation (such as urges to urinate); unfinished business from our current lives; and the resonances these contemporary stresses have with foundational issues with which we have struggled since our earliest years. Working on these four fronts, nocturnal mentation has the complex task of trying to shield us from disturbing stimuli and "knit up the raveled sleeve of care," as Shakespeare so elegantly phrased it, in order to facilitate restorative sleep. Dreams have other important functions as well but, fascinating though they are, it would be tangential to our current goals to venture into those purposes at this point.

Sometimes dreams are unable to put to rest or otherwise resolve our intense stresses, intrapsychic dilemmas, and the residua emanating from developmental trauma. When these challenges exceed the dream's capabilities, nightmares may ensue. In such instances, a psychic function that Freud charmingly called *the night watchman* may wake us up. This security officer's role is to free us from the hallucinatory realm of the nightmare. "Thank God that was just a dream!" we sigh with profound relief. Fervently we hope we will not re-enter that terrifying domain when we go back to sleep. "Now I lay me down to sleep. I pray the Lord my soul to keep. If I should die before I wake … " Hopefully before we meet any such terminal fate in a nightmare, the watchman will sound the alarm, rousing us back to the land of the living.

When dreaming works well, we can act out even our most dangerous impulses because the mind has been disconnected from motility. Paul, a very likeable adolescent patient, provides an excellent illustration of this fortunate phenomenon. He was extremely reluctant to share with me a profoundly upsetting dream he had experienced the night before. The fact that he mentioned having had such a dream was, no doubt, a good sign that at least a small part of him wanted to share that he had an inner life, one that could be discombobulating. Eventually, with great hesitation, horror, and self-loathing, this fine young man, his eyes averted in alarm and shame, gasped that in his dream: "I slit my younger sister's throat with a kitchen carving knife!" This grotesque image shook Paul to the core. His face contorted in shock as if he had actually committed this crime in reality. Of course, with his access to motility securely disabled, he caused no actual harm to anyone.

Paul quickly wrote this deeply unsettling dream off as being the meaningless result of having deviated from his rigorous, health-conscious diet. He had gone out and consumed some beer with a friend several hours before going to bed that night. The alcohol, he was sure, had caused this dreadful dream. I suggested this nocturnal horror 'movie' in which he starred might not be meaningless. It could be letting us know just how angry he can sometimes feel toward Paula, the 'golden child' of his nuclear family to whom everything, such as health, popularity, and academic success, always seemed to come so easily. Only in this dream state, with access to motility firmly blocked, could Paul allow himself to be aware of the extent of his envy and hostility toward his also beloved sibling, and begin to understand why he felt that way. From this perspective his dream, while profoundly upsetting, was also potentially enlightening, and useful for expanding his self-awareness and increasing his ability to tolerate and manage complicated thoughts, intense feelings, and extreme fantasies. Paul agreed that this perspective on his nightmare made sense. Nonetheless, he clearly still felt absolutely awful that he could have generated such a repugnant script, even in a harmless dream.

Just as dreams cannot always contain and manage all our concerns so that we can comfortably continue sleeping, so, too, the night watchman may not always succeed in waking us up fully from a nightmare. On such occasions, it may seem as if this security officer were dozing on the job. In some such instances of suboptimal psychic functioning, our access to motility may not be fully disconnected, or it may be restored to some extent while we continue to be trapped in our nightmare. We may then thrash about in our sleep, yell, or even leap out of bed to engage in some form of flight or fight behavior aimed at saving ourselves and perhaps our loved ones from whatever was threatening us in our dream.

When Kenneth Parks headed out a sixth floor window in his sleep when he was a preteen, the switch on his access to motility was clearly not in the 'off' position. Fortunately his mother, who was still up and about and checking to make sure her son was sleeping safely and soundly, managed to grab him by his leg before he fell several storeys to the ground below. Had she not been on duty as an external night watchman, Ken would have seriously injured or killed himself. Unfortunately, years later, when he was a young adult, no one was there to seize him as he left his home to *sleepdrive* to his in-laws'. Nor was anybody there to restrain him twenty-five minutes later when he brutally assaulted his wife's parents. It was equally tragic that there was nobody to securely hold Oscar Pistorius during what I will argue was his parasomniac episode.

Due to their immature nervous systems, children are prone to sleepwalking, sleeptalking, and sleep terrors (pavor nocturnus). In the latter condition, they appear to be having nightmares from which they cannot easily be woken. Typically they sit up abruptly during these episodes and scream, as if they are terrified of something. They may after awhile fall back to sleep, or run about with a high heart rate in a glassy-eyed frenzy of escape-like activity. If parents attempt to console and control their offspring during such events, these children will stay stiff and distraught. They may even beat with their fists on their parents' bodies. Youngsters have full or partial *amnesia* for all these episodes that arise during deep non-REM sleep. On rare occasions, a single image may be recalled.

Pavor nocturnus may continue from childhood into maturity. Alternatively, it may begin in adulthood. More than two percent of adults have sleep terrors up to age sixty-five, after which the prevalence drops to one percent. (Approximately 4% of adults sleepwalk.) These nocturnal terrors are characterized by sudden, loud, terrified screaming, with wide dilation of the pupils, rapid heart rate and breathing, and profuse sweating. The person may sit up quickly while shouting or yelling. They may engage in frenzied activity and become injured. There is usually a fight or flight theme in relation to perceived attack.

What Is This Thing Called Parasomnia?

Professor Carlos Schenck defines parasomnia as referring to all the abnormal things that can happen to people while they sleep, apart from sleep apnea. Some examples he describes as belonging to this diagnostic category are: sleepwalking; sleep-related eating disorder; nightmares; sleep paralysis; rapid eye movement (REM) sleep behavior disorder (RBD); sleep aggression; and sexsomnia, sometimes called sleepsex or atypical sexual behaviors of sleep (sexual acts carried out by sleepers usually during confusional arousals but sometimes during somnambulism). The parasomniac category of sleepwalking also covers other peculiar behaviors such as sleepdriving and other instances where individuals carry out surprisingly complex and often self-endangering activities. One sleep researcher, Rosalind Cartwright, has noted the surprisingly high frequency of sleep emailing. Parasomnias form a nebulous realm of disturbed sleep and dreaming, Professor Schenck (2005) notes. Individuals with these conditions suffer from "massive, radical transformations emanating from deep within. ... Their brains are misfiring during sleep, resulting in aberrant behavior, distorted perception, and altered dreaming" (p. 12). Since these parasomnias frequently run in families, there is probably often a genetic factor. Brain disorders may be responsible, as in many cases of REM sleep behavior disorder (discussed more fully later). Parasomnias may be triggered by other sleep disorders such as obstructive sleep apnea, and by various medications. These nocturnal oddities affect approximately ten percent of Americans. Occurring at all ages, they are most common in children.

Parasomnias can occur at any point in the sleep cycle. If they manifest while falling asleep, people may experience disturbing hallucinations or sleep paralysis where they are unable to move for seconds or minutes. Here access to motility has been shut off while waking consciousness continues. This paralysis can be frightening, especially when accompanied by disturbing hallucinations.

Parasomnias that occur during sleep include nightmares, sleep-related groaning that can prevent roommates from sleeping, and REM sleep behavior disorder (RBD) that often involves vigorous, harmful, *dream-enacting* behaviors. RBD dreams are not usually ordinary. Typically they are much more vivid, intense, physically active, confrontational, aggressive, and violent, with classic fight or flight scenarios. While these individuals dream of attacking and trying to kill intruders, or fighting off wild animals, usually their bedmates are the recipients of these assaults. Those with this disorder may yell and shout profanities. They are at high risk for injuring themselves or their partners, sometimes fatally. Most people with RBD remember the dreams they enacted, although at least ten percent do not.

These agitated parasomniacs may: punch through

walls; crash through glass windows, plummeting to the ground below; forcefully drag someone out of bed, trying to save them from imaginary attack; hurt someone who is usually asleep but is mistaken for the attacker; pick up weapons; check under beds and in closets; create barricades; smash lamps and other nearby appliances; and throw things at invisible intruders. These terrified actors generally remember nothing about these events. If they do, it is typically a vague sense of fright, or a hazy image of something chasing them, or of some frightening entity being in the room.

The average age of onset of chronic RBD is in the early 50's, predominantly (85%) in males. These conditions can, however, manifest in either sex, at virtually any age. It is possible that as many females as males may have RBD, but with less violence, in accord with general trends observed in male-female comparisons. These quieter forms of RBD would not cause as many problems and therefore would remain under-reported. They would be less likely to instigate medical or psychological interventions.

Professor Schenck's first RBD patient, Donald Dorff, described one of his episodes as a *"violent moving nightmare."* Another time he believed he was engaged in a vigorous football game. In the middle of that dream, he woke up, finding himself lying on the floor. He had smashed into his dresser, knocking everything off the top and shattering the mirror.

RBD can affect people taking certain medications, such as antidepressants. It can manifest in individuals who have, or are at risk for developing neurological disorders, such as Parkinson's, narcolepsy, or stroke. With regard to medications, in Oscar Pistorius' bedroom police found needles and boxes of what they believed to be testosterone. The prosecution wondered whether this substance could have fueled irritability and aggressiveness. The defense countered that the substance was merely an herbal remedy, Testis Compositum, which athletes use to help repair muscle tissue. Ben Greenfield, an expert in fitness, nutrition, and sports science, explained in Fox News Magazine on February 21, 2017 that Testis Compositum is a blend of purported testosterone-enhancing compounds like pig testicles, heart, embryo and adrenal gland. It can contain other ingredients like cortisone, ginseng, botanicals, and minerals.

What Steven Lamm, director of men's health at New York University's School of Medicine, found most interesting was that the name of this substance "implies it aids with testosterone production." In homeopathic doses, as Testis Compositum is used, the likelihood of stimulating testosterone production is extremely low, Dr. Lamm asserted. Ben Greenfield agreed: "The stuff can help with sexual performance and also can help you feel a little better if you have very low testosterone, but you'd actually have to take enormous quantities of something like Testis Compositum to get a significant performance-enhancing effect." It's not a banned substance either, noted Dr. Lamm. "The fact that [the Olympic Committee] didn't appear to have any problems with the substance tells me that it doesn't do anything."

The use of Testis Compositum may be indicative of something more serious, Ben Greenfield opined: "Most athletes use this as a 'cover up' for use of the stuff that really works: bioidentical testosterone and DHEA creams, lotions and injections." As for the needles found in Oscar's home, "At least in America—I don't know how it is in other countries—you can't, as a consumer, buy anything over the counter that is injectable," says Dr. Lamm.

Greenfield and Lamm concurred that Testis Compusitum would have little, if any, effect on an athlete. With Olympic athletes, their testosterone, 99.9 percent of the time, is completely normal, Lamm states. Low testosterone is usually a symptom among men with poor health. "If I'm looking at a conditioned athlete, with 10 percent body fat, the likelihood they have low testosterone is zero." He dismissed the notion that Testis Compositum had an effect on Oscar on the night of the murder. "No matter what medication, they'll always try to connect it to something," he states, referring to the media. He doubted there was much substance to such speculation.

Other parasomnias (confusional arousals, sleepwalk-ing, sleep terrors, sleep-related eating disorder) can occur when sleepers have abrupt, partial awakenings. When people are waking up, sleep-related hallucinations can happen, Professor Brogaard & Kristian Marlow note. As Kenneth Parks began to emerge from his somnambulism and saw his mother-in-law's face as sad, he may have been in a hallucinatory state of mind. Reports from other somnambulists suggest that hallucinations or dream-like states of mind take place during their perambulations. Brogaard & Marlow cite one close call in which Alyson Bair, a 31-year-old woman from Idaho, had a nightmare that she was in a deep river, getting tired. In her dream she realized she actually was drowning. Suddenly she woke up—perhaps a manifestation of Freud's night watchman being on the job. Alyson had been sleepwalking, ending up in the river outside her home. "I thought I was dreaming, but then I realized I wasn't and I was scared," she told ABC News. Making her way to the riverbank, she stayed put until she was found the next morning. These confusions between sleeping, waking, dreaming, hallucinating, and reality perception, I will argue, were likely also operative during Oscar Pistorius' nocturnal episode that, tragically, went beyond Alyson's near death experience.

In a more dangerous version of Alyson's aqueous incident, the Associated Press reported on Nov. 27, 1998 that James Currens, a seventy-seven-year-old man in Palm Harbor, Florida with a habit of sleepwalking, awoke in several feet of water in a pond behind his home. His legs were stuck in the mud. James recalled several alligators coming around him. Attempting to keep them away, he poked at them with his cane. A neighbor heard him yelling and called the police. Officers used lights to scare off the alligators and rescued James.

PART III

RADICAL SCIENTIFIC RE-VIEW OF OSCAR'S CRIME AND CONVICTION

Chapter 10

PERJURY IN PRETORIA?

Apparent suicide ...assault, or murder ... may be the unintentional, nonculpable but catastrophic result of disorders of arousal, sleep-related seizures, RBD [rapid eye movement sleep behavior disorder], or psychogenic dissociative states. The majority of these conditions are diagnosable and, more importantly, are treatable. The social and legal implications are obvious.
                                    —Mahowald et al.,
                    Handbook of Clinical Neurology

In this Section, I will explore how what we know from the psychology and neurophysiology of sleep and dreaming offers an enormous amount of extremely valuable insight toward elucidating what likely happened in Oscar Pistorius' home on Saint Valentine's Day, 2013. Without the profound understanding these fields of scientific inquiry provide, we would be left with a case with so many aspects that make absolutely no sense that the event would have to be regarded, disconcertingly, as forever unsolved.

Pictures Do Not Lie ...or Do They?

At Oscar's trial, Police Photograph #68 became the

focus of intense debate. Its depiction of the crime scene did not support the Blade Runner's version of what had transpired. Responding to these discrepancies, Oscar charged that the police had extensively tampered with the scene, rearranging numerous items.

If a witness can show that detectives have altered a situation in order to prove their case, that demonstration of wrongdoing might help acquit the defendant. Since Oscar always admitted he was the one who had fired the bullets into the toilet chamber, police officers would not have had any motive for rearranging anything to increase the likelihood of conviction. Consequently, in light of this photographic evidence, Oscar's account of what happened between him and his lover was simply a lie, the prosecution pronounced.

Oscar had claimed that he got out of bed in the middle of the night in question to bring in two fans from the balcony doorway. Earlier on that warm African evening he had placed them in the doorway to cool the bedroom. One was mounted on a tall metal tripod. The other, a small black fan, was positioned beneath that three-legged stand. After bringing both cooling devices in, Oscar closed the balcony door and the blinds and curtains—at least that is what he maintained.

Contra this account, in the Police Photograph, the large tripod fan was still in the balcony doorway after the crime. To resolve these discrepant facts, Oscar insisted police put the stand-up fan back in the doorway. "The fan could not possibly be there, because it is in the way of the door's opening. ...I would have run out on to the balcony My Lady and where I shouted for help, that fan would have been in the way. So it was ... " Before he could complete that sentence, prosecutor Gerrie Nel interrupted aggressively: "It never happened. ...That fan in the position where it is there, would have blocked you ...would have made it difficult for you to close that door." Nel was alleging Oscar never brought the fans in, never closed the door, blinds, or curtains, and never ran out onto the balcony to call for help since the fan would have barred his way. In the prosecutor's eyes, Oscar was simply a lying murderer.

There were other discrepancies between the photograph and Oscar's story. He had said the small fan had been plugged into the same adapter as the tall one. A picture showed the little fan, unplugged, far from the adapter. "This is not where I moved the fan that evening. I do not walk and put the fan in the corner of the room with the plug out," Oscar insisted, endeavoring to strengthen his case that detectives had relocated items.

One photograph showed hair clippers plugged into the adapter. There was no third opening for the small fan. Reconsidering his account in light of this evidence, Oscar suggested the small fan might have been plugged in behind his bedside table. He also suggested he might have tripped over the cord, unplugging the fan that, earlier, he had said he had deliberately disconnected and brought into the room. He did not actually remember tripping and never earlier mentioned stumbling over anything.

The State pointed out that the duvet on the floor would have been in Oscar's path as he moved in the dark to the bathroom. He insisted that comforter had always been on the bed, never on the floor. He had seen it on Reeva when he got up and later observed it on the bed after the shooting when he was putting on his prosthetic legs. The police, he insisted, had moved the eiderdown. (Agitated parasomniacs often kick or throw blankets off their beds – a possibility we will discuss later.)

Oscar had claimed that after having brought in the fans and closing the doors and blinds, he had been about to place Reeva's jeans over a small LED light to make the room even darker in order to optimize conditions for a good night's rest. In the middle of that act, he heard a sound in the bathroom. He dropped her jeans so he could investigate. The State pointed out that the jeans were found on top of the duvet, indicating the comforter had been on the floor prior to Oscar's dropping the pants on it. The defense argued that Reeva's jeans might only have looked like they were on top of the duvet. In actuality, they may simply have been in close proximity to it. A trail of blood drops led up to and onto the eiderdown, providing a chain of evidence that further contradicted the Blade Runner's insistence that the duvet had always been on the bed.

"Mr. Pistorius, your version is a lie," Nel charged. To some observers' astonishment, Oscar agreed that if the fans, duvet, and jeans had truly been in the positions portrayed in the pictures, his version of events could not be true. Even as a mere possibility, that was quite an admission.

Oscar's seemingly implausible assertion of investigative malfeasance provides a good illustration of how our minds attempt to come up with 'logical' explanations for otherwise inexplicable or contradictory facts. Recall Kenneth Parks' story that someone must have broken into his home, drugged his Kool-Aid, then drove him to his in-laws' residence. There, he reasoned, upon coming to his senses, he must have tried to protect his wife's parents from the assailant, severely injuring his hands in this heroic endeavor. We are programmed to do the best we can to weave encompassing, credible narratives to make sense of whatever data we have. These productions may contain holes of varying, and sometimes huge, magnitude.

Responding to Oscar's allegations that detectives tampered with the crime scene, Prosecutor Nel stated with extreme sarcasm: "Now we have to look for a policeman that did the following: that moved the duvet to the carpet, that moved the fan back, that moved the curtain open. Those three things, am I right?" Sticking to his story, Oscar replied: "That is correct." He claimed expert witnesses would support his assertion. No specialist the defense subsequently called upon ever spoke of modifications being made to the placement of these items.

What are we to make of these gross discrepancies between Oscar's account and the photograph? The prosecution believed the accused was simply an untrustworthy dissembler, rigidly adhering to his completely implausible story, modifying it as needed to fit inconvenient facts the state presented. Oscar insisted on his narrative, charging that the police were the ones guilty of falsification. We will soon see there is an alternative, third explanation that could account for these radical contradictions.

In Sigmund Freud's 24-volume oeuvre, *The Interpretation of Dreams* is arguably his most significant contribution. Many consider this seminal text to be the most important book ever written in psychology. In this work, Freud described a subtype of nocturnal mentation that he referred to as *dreams of convenience*. These reveries portray some necessary action as having been fulfilled. Consequently, one does not have to interrupt one's sleep to attend to that pesky task. For example, if my bladder pushes for relief, I may dream I am urinating into a toilet. This 'hallucination' makes it unnecessary for me to interrupt my slumber. Our capacity to generate dreams of convenience seems to have been selected in the course of evolution due to its ability to preserve the restorative rest that is so crucial for physical and mental health.

In parasomnias in which access to motility is not disconnected, dreams of convenience can spill into reality. Unlike those who merely dream that they are urinating, Kenneth Parks' grandfather used to get up in the middle of the night and empty his bladder in the closet. He is far from the only person to have sought relief in that fashion. Needless to say, there is initially great surprise and concern about this deviation from good toilet training in the families of these parasomniacs.

Police Photograph #68 suggests to me that in relation to the stand-up fan in the balcony doorway (and all other contested, crime scene details), Oscar was likely involved in a dream of convenience. Before going to sleep, it was on his mind that he had left the fans running. Supposedly Reeva had assured him she would turn them, the lights, and the television set off before coming to bed. He may not have believed she would remember, or she might have decided to leave the fans on. Oscar might then have heard, or imagined, these devices still humming during his sleep. His continuing subconscious attention to them may also have reflected his concern that criminals could enter his home through the open balcony door. This portal would have afforded a much more accessible entry point than the bathroom window.

Hearing or dreaming of the fans humming, and simultaneously not wanting to wake up and get out of bed to turn them off, Oscar may simply have *dreamt* he performed those actions. This scenario would account for Police Photograph #68 showing the fan in the doorway with the blinds and curtains open, and for Oscar's conviction concerning the exact opposite 'facts'. From this viewpoint, based on scientific understanding of sleep and dreaming, neither he nor the police were lying. The photographs could have been highly accurate and Oscar's version may have been an equally precise portrayal of the events he experienced and perceived—while immersed in a dream of convenience.

With regard to the wandering duvet, prior to and even during Oscar's dream of convenience, Reeva would still have been sleeping comfortably beside him. Her legs, if not her entire body, would have been resting peacefully under that comforter. Consequently he would insist that he saw it on Reeva when he imagined he got out of bed to attend to the fans. Oscar's adamant stance that the duvet never left the bed suggests he was caught in the compelling psychic reality of his dream in which the comforter was always at least partially covering his lover while he had merely slipped out from under it to attend to the fans, door, curtains, LED light, blinds, and so forth. In reality, as captured in the police photograph, the eiderdown had either slipped onto the floor or had been pushed there, perhaps because the room was so warm that the lovers no longer required that extra insulation, or it could have been kicked off the bed during Oscar's agitated state that will soon be described.

Oscar claimed he had been operating in total darkness while bringing in the fans, closing the door, curtains, blinds, and so on. This absence of light accounted for his not seeing Reeva getting up and going to the toilet. The fact that the LED light was on and, in addition, the photograph indicated the blinds and drapes were partly open suggests that he had not been functioning in complete blackness. Furthermore, his previous girlfriend, Samantha Taylor, shared in an interview that there was always some light on in his bedroom. The curtains were always "fairly open," she said. It may, nonetheless, have seemed very dark if Oscar's eyes were wide shut as he participated in a dream of convenience. If in his dream he had closed all the blinds and curtains, the room would have been experienced as very dark. These possibilities could account both for his assertion that the room had been pitch black, hence he would not have been able to see Reeva heading for the bathroom, and the photograph indicating the drapes and curtains were open, allowing some light to enter. Once again, the idea that Oscar had been experiencing a dream of convenience supports the likelihood that neither he nor the police were being deceitful.

After discovering he had killed Reeva, Oscar may well have screamed for help as he claimed. Several neighbors attested to having heard shouts that night. Based on expert testimony, Judge Masipa did not think the neighbors' accounts could be taken at face value. In any case, the police photograph of the stand-up fan in the doorway suggests that Oscar did not run out onto the balcony to yell for assistance as he maintained. He may have been in a state of confusional arousal, alternating betwixt dream and reality, with one foot in each realm. In this lingering oneiric state in which he believed he had removed the fan from the doorway, he could easily have gone out onto the balcony to cry for help. In reality, with the fan blocking that exit, he would have had to shout from inside the bedroom. A parasomniac hypothesis concerning alternating degrees of awareness, being simultaneously and sequentially conscious and unconscious, allows for both Oscar's conviction that he ran onto the balcony to scream for assistance and for the police picture indicating he could not have done so.

From the binary perspective that characterized the courtroom proceedings, either Oscar was lying or the police had altered the crime scene. Neither point of view seems very plausible. There was no compelling reason for Oscar to lie about the fans, duvet, drapes, blinds, jeans, going out onto the balcony, and other details. He would have wanted to present himself as a truthful person who made an honest, horrific mistake when he felt moved to fire that fateful volley of bullets into the toilet chamber. Similarly, the police would have no compelling motive to rearrange items in the bedroom since they already had the confession they needed from Oscar.

While Oscar's assertion of police malfeasance does not seem very probable, what does seem believable is the alternative, third perspective, that he was accurately portraying the things that he saw and did—while ensconced in a dream state. That 'hallucinatory' frame of mind would, of course, differ from reality. There is no reason to postulate him lying. This idea that he was involved in a dream of convenience is sufficiently powerful to explain *all* the discrepancies between his version of events that evening versus those portrayed in the photographs. From this scientific perspective, Oscar was not mendacious and the police were not perfidious. With this hypothesis, all parties appear in a much better light than was possible during the courtroom crossfire of mutual accusations.

Chapter 11

The Bail Magistrate's and the Judge's Profound Puzzlement

Two questions accompany each case of purported sleep-related violence: (1) Is it possible for behavior this complex to have arisen in a mixed state of wakefulness and sleep without conscious awareness or responsibility for the act? and (2) Is that what happened at the time of the incident? The answer to the first is usually "yes." The second can never be determined with surety after the fact.
—Mahowald et al., *Handbook of Clinical Neurology*

Let us re-read Oscar's application for bail in which he described what had transpired on that dreadful morning of Saint Valentine's Day, 2013. This time, armed with our ideas concerning dreams and parasomnias, we will examine his description from a radically different perspective than anyone has utilized. We will consider his affidavit with the possibility in mind that rather than simply describing actuality, he might have been reporting from a state of dreaming (a dream of convenience) and parasomnia (e.g., nightmare, sleep terror, confusional arousal, rapid eye movement sleep behavior disorder, dream enactment), only slowly coming fully to his senses toward the end of the fatal incident.

As Oscar was about to place Reeva's jeans over the little LED light to make the bedroom darker, he reports he heard a sound. He "realized that someone was in the bathroom." In the previous chapter I provided evidence supporting the idea that he had not really been awake and out of bed attending to fans, blinds, curtains, and LED lights. It seemed likely he was doing those things during a dream of convenience. While still in that oneiric state, when he heard a sound emanating from the bathroom, he instantly 'real-ized' intruders had entered his home. In this manner, a thought became an immediate psychic 'reality' while he was still in a dream state – albeit a dream that was rapidly becoming a nightmare.

If Oscar had been operating in accord with normal waking life reasoning, he would have realized that the most likely person to have been in the bathroom would, of course, have been Reeva. He would simply have checked to see if she were in his bed. If she were not, he would deduce that she had made that bathroom noise.

In contrast to the simple inference that it was Reeva in the bathroom, it would be exceedingly difficult for criminals to penetrate the exclusive, gated, Silver Woods Country Estates where Oscar resided. Not only did he have an alarm system in his home, but also a twelve-foot high perimeter wall with a guarded, access-controlled entrance surrounded the Estate. Underground sensors ringed the compound. There were security cameras, closed circuit television, and round-the-clock patrols. Additionally, Oscar had a pit bull and a bull terrier that would have surely barked, even if they had not been trained as attack dogs.

In this well secured environment, Oscar rightly relaxed and drifted off to dreamland. Consciously he knew he was quite safe. As he shifted into his unconscious, inner world, his situation became very different. From what was likely a simple dream of convenience in which he was bringing in the fans, he transitioned precipitously into a parasomniac state (e.g., nightmare, night terror, rapid eye movement sleep behavior disorder). Instead of taking the obviously indicated action of checking to see whether Reeva was still in bed:

> I felt a sense of terror rushing over me. There are no burglar bars across the bathroom window and I knew that contractors who worked at my house had left the ladders outside. Although I did not have my prosthetic legs on I have mobility on my stumps. I believed that someone had entered my house. I was too scared to switch a light on. I grabbed my 9mm pistol from underneath my bed. On my way to the bathroom I screamed words to the effect for him/them to get out of my house and for Reeva to phone the police. It was pitch dark in the bedroom and I thought Reeva was in bed.

Oscar's dream of convenience in which he was attending to the fans, then covering the LED light with his sleeping girlfriend's jeans seemed to have morphed into what one Professor Schenck's (2005) patient referred to as an "instant nightmare. ...It's a normal dream and it very suddenly goes bad" (p. 96). For Schenck's patient, machine guns would suddenly emerge from the wall and shoot at him. Using similar 'instant nightmare' language while out on bail, Oscar stated that "instant fear" drove him to grab his gun. Similar to Professor Schenck's patient, Oscar seemed to be sliding rapidly down the slippery slope from his dream of convenience via an instant nightmare to a complex form of dream enactment with varying degrees of consciousness and reality orientation. His instant nightmare was becoming similar to what Dr. Schenck's first patient, Donald Dorff, called "violent moving nightmares." Some features of higher level cognitive functioning were present while others were not available to Oscar. The 'night watchman' had somewhat succeeded and partially failed to wake him up.

> I noticed that the bathroom window was open. I realized that the intruder/s was/were in the toilet because the toilet door was closed and I did not see anyone in the bathroom. [BW: *In his nightmare state of mind, Oscar remains convinced there are home invaders. His mind is not open to alternative possibilities, as he would have been had he been awake, such as the likelihood that it would have been Reeva in the toilet stall.*] I heard movement inside the toilet. The toilet is inside the bathroom and has a separate door. It filled me with horror and fear of an intruder or intruders being inside the toilet. [BW: *In the 'delusional' nightmare state, it cannot occur to Oscar that it could be Reeva in the toilet.*]

> I thought he or they [BW: *not she*] must have entered through the unprotected window. [BW: *In real life reasoning, it would be easier for burglars to enter through the balcony door that was open according to Police Photograph #68. In Oscar's dream world, however, he had closed that door. Therefore, intruders would have to enter via the window, even though police did not believe such ingress possible.*] As I did not have my prosthetic legs on and felt extremely vulnerable, I knew I had to protect Reeva and myself. I believed that when the intruder/s came out of the toilet we would be in grave danger.

> I felt trapped as my bedroom door was locked [BW: *In reality, Oscar could have unlocked it.*] and I have limited mobility on my stumps. I fired shots at the toilet door and shouted to Reeva

to phone the police. She did not respond and I moved backwards out of the bathroom, keeping my eyes on the bathroom entrance. Everything was pitch dark in the bedroom [*BW: Although in reality the LED light was on and the curtains and blinds were partly open.*] and I was still too scared to switch on a light. Reeva was not responding. When I reached the bed, I realized that Reeva was not in bed.

At last, Oscar seems to have started waking up from what I believe to have been a state of dream enactment, a 'violent moving nightmare'. His normally accurate, invaluable, reality awareness, reality testing, and reasoning abilities were returning. Suddenly the entire situation was looking very different. With a jolt, he realized Reeva was not responding to him. She was not even in the bedroom.

That is when it dawned on me that it could have been Reeva who was in the toilet. [*BW: Now back in waking consciousness, he was able to figure that out immediately.*] I returned to the bathroom calling her name. I tried to open the toilet door but it was locked. I rushed back into the bedroom and opened the sliding door exiting onto the balcony and screamed for help. I put on my prosthetic legs, ran back to the bathroom and tried to kick the toilet door open. I think I must then have turned on the lights.

I went back into the bedroom and grabbed my cricket bat to bash open the toilet door. A panel or panels broke off and I found the key on the floor and unlocked and opened the door. Reeva was slumped over but alive. I battled to get her out of the toilet and pulled her into the bathroom.

I phoned Johan Stander ("Stander") who was involved in the administration of the estate and asked him to phone the ambulance. I phoned Netcare and asked for help. I went downstairs to open the front door. I returned to the bathroom and picked Reeva up as I had been told not to wait for the paramedics, but to take her to hospital. I carried her downstairs in order to take her to the hospital. On my way down Stander arrived. [*BW: Oscar is now fully awake. He performs a series of appropriate actions in a fully rational manner, even though he is in great emotional distress.*]

A doctor who lives in the complex also arrived. Downstairs, I tried to render the assistance to Reeva that I could, but she died in my arms. I am absolutely mortified by the events and the devastating loss of my beloved Reeva.

In keeping with the idea that auditory stimulation (such as humming fans or bathroom activity) can trigger dreams, nightmares, or night terrors, during the trial Oscar stated: "I *heard* a window open in the bathroom. It *sounded* like the window sliding open and then I could *hear* the window hit the frame as if it had slipped to a point where it cannot slide any more. ...That is the moment that everything changed" [*italics added*]. Indeed. That sound, whether real, misperceived, or merely imagined, seems to have triggered a chain of parasomniac events.

A photograph of the crime scene confirmed that the bathroom window was open. We do not know if it had been open all along or whether Reeva opened it when she went to the bathroom. In any event, rather than having a benevolent dream turn that noise into something innocuous or pleasant, like the sound of wooden drum sticks, Oscar interpreted it in the most threatening way possible. Sliding swiftly into a nightmarish state, he sprung into defensive dream action that spilled into reality. Motility was available, even if some higher order cognitive functions were not. Most mothers awaken when their child cries, even from another room. They have an added sort of night watchman beyond the one that Freud described that arouses us from nightmares. This maternal security officer does not sleep or, at most, slumbers with one ear open. She is attuned to certain important signals, such as her baby's cry. When she detects a relevant stimulus, this guard wakens the mother so she can attend to the situation, taking whatever actions might be indicated.

When Oscar heard that bathroom sound, one could say his analogous night watchman—attuned not to crying babies but to home invaders—was functioning in hypersensitive high gear. That guard instantly sounded an alarm, prompting Oscar to spring to attention and take decisive action. Unfortunately, this protective nocturnal presence may not have been able to fully arouse the sleeper whom he was trying to help. Instead of Oscar waking up and determining whether there was any real danger, he appears to have slipped from his dream of convenience into a nightmare in which he was sure the sound was real and indicative of grave danger. He was convinced his home had been invaded, rather than that idea merely being a disturbing possibility that required waking up and investigation, very likely involving quick consultation with Reeva before taking any further, potentially dangerous steps.

Judge Thokozile Matilda Masipa's Four Questions

Having begun to consider Oscar's account from the perspective of dreaming and parasomnia, we can now usefully return to the several glaring issues that Judge Masipa found so profoundly puzzling. First, she wondered, "Why the accused did not ascertain from the deceased when he heard the window open, whether she too had heard anything?"

If Oscar had been awake and operating in accord with what Freud called rational, *secondary process thinking*, he no doubt would have nudged Reeva, checking with her as to whether she, too, had heard a sound. That course of action would have been eminently reasonable and expected. In dream states, in contrast, where *primary process* cognition predominates, there are often all sorts of gaps, contradictions, and seemingly illogical occurrences. Having transitioned from a benevolent dream of convenience to a malevolent nightmare, Oscar did not have his usual, more sophisticated cognitive capacities available to him. Ensconced in the modus operandi of nocturnal mentation, he could not behave in the wise manner that Judge Masipa (and we and he) would have wanted him to act, that is in all the ways in which he would have functioned had he been fully awake. In threatening dreams, one bolts into fight or flight mode. Action trumps reflective, logical thought. The dreaming and parasomnia hypotheses thus provide clear answers to Judge Masipa's first query as to why Oscar did not do the logical thing one would normally expect, namely consult his lover before heading off to a potentially lethal confrontation several steps down the hall from the bed.

In contrast to how Oscar acted during what I believe was a dream enactment, when he was in his normal frame of mind he is known to have always behaved very differently. When not in a parasomniac state, he consistently acted exactly as Judge Masipa would have expected. In an interview, his previous girlfriend, Samantha Taylor, noted that whenever they were sleeping together and Oscar heard a sound, he always asked if she, too, had heard it. If she had, they could then discuss what the noise might have been before checking it out further, or simply going back to sleep.

Judge Masipa's second perplexing question follows closely from her first one: "Why he did not ascertain whether the deceased had heard him since he did not get a response from the deceased before making his way to the bathroom?" In real life, this would be an obvious, relevant query and expectation. If Oscar had not been in a dream or parasomniac state, he would no doubt have made sure Reeva was awake and had heard him telling her he was going to check out the bathroom noise, that she should call the police, etc. He would have made sure his urgent dictates had registered clearly with her before proceeding to confront dangerous intruders. In a dream state, we do not necessarily think of and bother ourselves with such important details. We are not in a logical, secondary process frame of mind. In a nightmare, fleeing from, or attempting to eliminate an imminent threat is all that matters. There is no time for other crucial considerations.

Not only would Oscar have checked with Reeva to make sure she had heard him, but she in turn would probably have cautioned him about going to the bathroom. She would have told him not to go there or, at the very least, would have warned him to be extremely careful. She might have urged him to take some safer, alternative course of action. She might have suggested they go out onto the balcony, shut the door behind them, call the Estate's security officers and police on their cell phones, scream for neighbors to come help them, and so forth. In contrast, rushing to emergency protective action, a terrified dreamer may skip over such logical steps that characterize normal interactions between caring, awake people. On the day and evening preceding the tragedy, Oscar and Reeva seem to have been communicating in exactly those ordinary, intimate, loving ways. In his dream, however, as in many other people's nocturnal mentation, some of those ordinary interpersonal subtleties were clearly lacking.

From the preceding considerations, it is clear that Judge Masipa's second query concerning why Oscar did not make sure Reeva was on the same page as he was is also very well addressed by the dreaming and parasomnia hypotheses. Judge Masipa's third penetrating question was: "Why the deceased was in the toilet and only a few metres away from the accused, did not communicate with the accused, or phone the police as requested by the accused. This the deceased could have done, irrespective of whether she was in the bedroom or in the toilet, as she had her cell phone with her. It *makes no sense* to say she did not hear him scream, 'get out'. It was the accused version that he screamed on top of his voice, when ordering the intruders to get out" [italics added].

Once again, the Judge's crucial query makes eminent sense—from the viewpoint of waking cognition. The situation she is interrogating and implicitly critiquing makes no sense whatsoever. Judge Masipa is proclaiming this fact loudly and clearly for all who have ears to hear and ponder. In order to generate a possible answer to her question, insights from the scientific understanding of the nature of dreaming and parasomnia are desperately needed. Seeking that solution, let us look at what Oscar told the Court about his hollering at Reeva and the burglars:

> As I entered where the passage is to the bathroom I was overcome with fear and started *screaming for the burglars to get out of my house. I shouted for Reeva to get on the floor.* ...I slowly made my way down the passage constantly aware that these people could come out at me any time. ...Just before I got to the wall where tiles start in the bathroom I stopped *shouting* as I was worried the person would know exactly where I was. I could get shot. I heard a toilet door slam. ...At this point I started *screaming again for Reeva to phone the police.* My eyes were going between the window and the toilet. I must have stood there for some time. I wasn't sure if someone was going to come out of the toilet and attack me or come up the ladder and point

a firearm in the house and start shooting. So I just stayed where I was and I *kept on screaming.* [*italics added*]

From all that hollering, Judge Masipa was completely correct in being profoundly baffled by the blatant impossibilities in Oscar's account. Reeva would certainly have responded to his high decibel bellowing at her, and at the imaginary intruders in the bathroom to get out. She would have reassured him that it was only she in the toilet chamber. On the other hand, if Oscar were only dreaming that he was screaming, Reeva would have heard nothing to which she could respond.

Recall Kenneth Parks thinking he had called out in concern to reassure his in-laws' frightened adolescent and young adult children who were hiding upstairs while he murdered their mother and assaulted their father. Ken insisted he yelled, "Kids, kids." Apparently he merely screamed these words in his dream. The children only heard him grunting like an animal, as people sometimes do while sleeping.

Even if Reeva had pleaded with Oscar to calm down and not fire his gun, to the extent that he was asleep, ensconced in a parasomniac state, he would not have heard her. The neighbors might have, but he would not, just as Kenneth Parks did not hear his in-laws yelling at him to stop assaulting them. Thus Judge Masipa's third query as to why Reeva neither responded to Oscar nor called the police as he ordered her to do is also well addressed by the dreaming and parasomnia hypotheses.

The Judge's fourth puzzlement concerned: "Why the accused fired not one, one shot but four shots, before he ran back to the bedroom to try to find the deceased." According to Oscar: "I fired shots at the toilet door and shouted to Reeva to phone the police. She did not respond." At last, he was starting to realize something was seriously amiss. This emerging awareness seems most likely due to the fact that he was finally beginning to wake up, perhaps due to having heard the loud shots he was firing, especially the fourth, final bullet blast.

Professor Rosalind Cartwright cites a case in which a married man kept a gun between the mattress and headboard of the couple's waterbed. This weapon had been purchased after prowlers were seen twice near their mobile home. Hearing this gun discharge while he was sleeping, he awoke. Unable to arouse his wife whom, it turned out, he had shot, he called the police. Just like that man's pistol woke him, Oscar's gunshots may have aroused him to the point that he was, at last, able to register that Reeva was not responding to his communications in the manner that Judge Masipa, Magistrate Nair, and anyone else in their right mind (that is, their awake mind) would expect. Now, finally, Oscar was also in that normal state of mind.

If one is open to the possibility that the Blade Runner was not in his usual consciousness but, rather, *dreamwalking*, prior to waking up and realizing Reeva was not responding to him, then it is no mystery that he did not stop at one shot. It is like how we may not wake up with the first ring of our alarm clocks or the first call from a family member to rise and start the day. It may take four or more loud sounds from an alarm clock, or from some other, much more powerful device, such as a pistol, before we emerge from our dream and begin to orient ourselves toward reality.

In keeping with the above considerations regarding how one can sleep through a single gunshot, on July 17, 1991, the Seattle Post-Intelligencer Times reported an Associated Press story in which a twenty-four-year-old sleepwalking sheriff's deputy grabbed his bedside pistol and shot himself in the leg during a dream in which he imagined he was struggling with someone. He did not realize he was wounded (parasomniac dissociative analgesia) until later when he awoke and saw blood. His wife also slept through the gunshot. Four bullets would probably have aroused both of them. Eventually this woman awoke, saw the condition of her spouse, and drove him to the hospital.

Like all Judge Masipa's previous questions, her fourth query about why Oscar fired not once, but four times is well addressed by the parasomnia hypothesis. In contrast, none of her crucial questions can be answered from the point of view of waking, logical, secondary process thought. If one is open to the likelihood that Oscar was in a dream state, then all four of the enormous mysteries that Judge Masipa identified dissolve. These enlightening explanations, based on the evolving science of sleep and dreaming, constitute compelling evidence that Oscar behaved in a state of dream enactment that night rather than in a rational, objective, waking manner.

From this scientific perspective, Oscar's dream began and ended with real world auditory events. First, he heard or imagined hearing, the fans in the balcony doorway. He may have handled that stimulus via a dream of convenience, visualizing that he brought them in. Next he heard a sound coming from the bathroom. This noise triggered a rapid transition from his dream of convenience into an instant nightmare related to his longstanding fear of home invaders. That nightmare may have further degenerated into sleep terror, rapid eye movement sleep behavior disorder, and confusional arousal. Unable to awaken Oscar by calling out to him, and before she could phone for help with the cellphone she held in her hand, Reeva succumbed to the bullets he blasted into the toilet chamber. When those loud cracks from his Parabellum woke him, he finally realized Reeva was not responding to his frantic calls. Having returned to waking consciousness, he could now quickly reason that she might have been the person he shot.

Recall Mark Pressman 's study in which he reported that all confusional arousals, 81% of sleep terrors, and 40 to 90% of sleepwalking cases were associated with provocations, including noise, touch and/or close proximity. In Oscar's case, sound figured prominently as an instigator of likely dreaming and parasomnia. In between the initiating and terminating auditory events, a steady stream of acoustic happenings occurred (dreamscreaming orders at Reeva and the home invaders, hearing threatening movement in the toilet stall).

Preceding Judge Masipa's articulation of these four, highly significant points pertaining to her profound puzzlement, Magistrate Desmond Nair had similarly noted near the end of Oscar's earlier bail hearing:

> I have difficulty in appreciating why the accused did not ascertain the whereabouts of his girlfriend when he got out of bed. I have difficulty in also coming to terms with the fact that the accused did not seek to verify who exactly was in the toilet when he could have asked. I also have difficulty in appreciating why the deceased would not have screamed back from the toilet. I have difficulty understanding why the deceased and the accused would not of like mind in those circumstances have escaped through the bedroom door than venture into the toilet. I have a problem also, as to why the accused would further venture into danger knowing full well that the intruder was in the toilet, leaving himself open to being attacked even before he shot.

The profound perplexities that Bail Magistrate Nair emphasized were not a nanometer closer to being understood after months of intense cross-examination, expert witnesses, and the Judge's lengthy deliberations after the court proceedings had concluded. These mysterious matters would remain forever incomprehensible—unless approached from a radically different viewpoint. Fortunately we now possess that needed perspective, thanks to the scientific understanding of dreaming and parasomnia. Examined from that penetrating vantage point, the incomprehensible becomes comprehensible.

The prosecution used these extreme improbabilities in Oscar's narrative to their benefit. Attorney Nel argued that in order to believe Oscar one would have to accept that Reeva got out of bed without saying a word to him while he was attending to the fans; that she slipped down the passageway without him seeing [or hearing] her; that she took her phone with her; and that she never once screamed when he shouted at the imaginary intruders. Furthermore, Nel asked, why would Oscar believe that an intruder who had just broken into his house would hide inside his toilet? "Your version is so improbable that nobody would ever believe it is reasonably, possibly true." For Nel, this incredulity constituted powerful evidence that Oscar was lying about what had happened, namely that he had argued with, and subsequently murdered Reeva in a fit of rage. Nel's objections, like the puzzlement of the Bail Magistrate and Judge, make eminent sense—if Oscar had been awake. If, however, he had been in a state of dream enactment, then the Blade Runner's version becomes very possibly true.

In *Chase Your Shadow: The Trials of Oscar Pistorius*, John Carlin reported that the public thought just like prosecutor Nel. "Who but a madman could imagine that a burglar would choose to lock himself inside a toilet? If Pistorius was not mad, he had to be lying," Carlin wrote. Neither Carlin nor the citizenry would know of a third, powerful, explanatory possibility, namely that Oscar was neither lying nor insane but, rather, had been in a state of dream enactment and confusional arousal.

Carlin chose the name for his book, *Chase Your Shadow*, from a piece of inspirational advice someone had given to Oscar regarding his athletic ambitions. That title now acquires an additional, ironic meaning with respect to parasomnia. On Saint Valentine's Day 2013, Oscar was chasing a shadowy projection from his dream world (dangerous home invaders). Tragically, that projection process eclipsed objective reality.

Chapter 12

KEY TO THE LOCKED DOOR

I suggest that somebody ...should, instead of writing a book called 'The Interpretation of Dreams,' write a book called 'The Interpretation of Facts,' translating them into dream language— not just as a perverse exercise, but in order to get a two-way traffic.

—Wilfrid Bion, British psychoanalyst

Weaving into his dream of convenience the sound that he interpreted as coming from intruders, Oscar might have subsequently slipped into a nightmare, then into dream enactment, possibly rapid eye movement sleep behavior disorder (RBD). To further understand this latter, peculiar condition, consider Brian Thomas, a sleepwalker, and his wife, Christine, holidaying in their camper in Britain in 2008. "Boy racers" woke them up. "As I went to sleep, it must have been on my mind that the camper wasn't secure. [*BW: just like Oscar was aware that his home was not impenetrable.*] Then—I don't know how much later it was—I recall seeing Chris in bed over the other side of the camper and someone on top of her. All I said was: 'You bastards, you got in here.' I grabbed this man round the neck and pulled him off." The following morning Brian woke up next to Christine's strangled, lifeless body. He phoned the police: "I think I've killed my wife. Oh my God. I thought someone had broken in, I must have been dreaming or something. His horror, remorse, and immediately turning himself in prefigured what Oscar would do five years later (as Kenneth Parks has also done). Deemed to have been acting under a *non-insane automatism*, like Kenneth Parks, Brian Thomas was acquitted. He had suffered night terrors for about fifty years without treatment. At the trailer park that night, Brian was not just experiencing non-REM pavor nocturnus. He was involved in rapid eye movement sleep behavior disorder (RBD).

Given the many cases in which dream enacting men, like Brian Thomas, have killed family members while believing they were defending them, one might reconsider Kenneth Parks' imagining he had been abducted to his in-laws' home where, beginning to return to consciousness, he tried to protect them from a killer. By secondary process standards, his theory was highly implausible. It is, however, conceivable that he, like Brian Thomas, Oscar, and so many others suffering from parasomnia might have dreamt he was endeavoring to protect people he loved from malevolent intruders. Subsequent to an experience that might have contained at least an element of *dreamwalking*, Ken may have accessed a vague dream memory trace remotely resembling the 'tall tale' he ultimately crafted to explain the otherwise incomprehensible events of that night.

After Kenneth resumed waking consciousness, at least to some degree, he heard his in-laws' offspring crying upstairs. He ran to reassure them. In a state of dream enactment and confusional arousal, he may have wanted to inform them that he had vanquished the killer, so they were all now safe. As Ken woke up further, he became aware that it was him who had killed his in-laws. Consequently he left their home to turn himself in to the police, just as Brian and Oscar did.

Another high-profile, non-insane automatism case concerned guitar player, Peter Buck. Ironically, Peter was part of a well-known American band called R.E.M. Their lead singer, Michael Stipe, named their group after the abbreviation for the rapid eye movement stage of sleep, a term he found in a random dictionary search. In 2002, Peter was acquitted of attacking staff on a transatlantic flight to London. The court accepted that he had no recollection of the incident because he was suffering from non-insane automatism at the time. His violence had been caused or facilitated by a combination of alcohol plus sleeping pill.

Many men suffering from sleep disorders have sexually or, in other ways, assaulted and, in worst cases, killed their bed partners. It is relatively easy to imagine that Oscar, dreaming like Brian Thomas that home invaders endangered him and his partner, might have slipped past a series of crucial psychic boundaries between ordinary dreaming, nightmare, and sleep terror (intense autonomic activation, sitting up, screaming, unresponsive to external stimuli). Before or after concerned Reeva attempted to waken him from his agitated state, he may have crossed yet another behavioral threshold—assaulting her in the hallucinatory conviction that she was the intruder, as so commonly happens in RBD. (Recall that the defense team's sleep experts at Kenneth Parks' trial hypothesized that his violence might have erupted when his in-laws tried to awaken him.)

Another of Professor Schenck's (2005) patients, Mel, reported a dream in which he was at his grandparents' farm, pitching hay with his grandfather. He asked his grandpa if he had noticed the buck and doe pass by the barn. Grandpa headed off to shoo those animals away. Mel told him he would stay put and try to get one of the creatures if they came back. When the doe returned, Mel rapped her on the neck with his pitchfork. She went down. Mel thought he could fix the situation by holding the animal's head and chin, giving her head a snap. In actuality, he had grabbed his wife's chin. She jumped and hollered, "What the hell are you trying to do?" Fortunately Mel heeded her shouts and woke up before any serious harm occurred, unlike Brian Thomas, Kenneth Parks, and Oscar.

Another woman whose husband suffered from RBD said he frequently grabbed her by the arm. "I have had an awful time getting away from him." On one occasion this man dreamt he was riding a motorcycle beside another motorcyclist who was trying to ram into him. He tried to kick the other motorcycle away. In reality, he was kicking his wife. "I got out of there quick," she reported: One can imagine Reeva needing to escape rapidly from a similarly assaultive, parasomniac Oscar.

Touching a dream enactor often triggers aggression. (Talking is less likely to precipitate violence.) As if such precipitous violence were not sufficiently terrifying, dream enactors can also experience incredible speed and strength, far exceeding that which they are capable of when awake. Professor Schenck (2007) described a young man with nocturnal dissociative disorder who believed he was a lion or tiger. In these identities, he could bite down on a mattress and drag it across the room with his teeth, or lift a marble table with his jaws.

Frightened by her lover's potentially lethal, parasomniac behavior, might Reeva have grabbed her cellphone and bolted to the bathroom—with Oscar in hot pursuit? To protect herself from this bewildering, frightening version of her beloved, she would understandably have slammed the door shut and locked it behind her, accounting for the otherwise unexplained loud closing and 'securing' of that barrier.

Oscar's previous girlfriend, Samantha Taylor, shared with an interviewer that she never locked the bathroom door when she went to the toilet during her many sleepovers with him. She could not imagine that anyone would bolt that barrier in the middle of the night. If the cubicle light were broken, as it apparently was, Samantha could not imagine anyone even closing the door. It is of course possible that

Reeva always locked bathroom doors, even during the night when no one else is awake, though such a habit does not seem very likely.

The prosecution was strongly convinced, along with many others, that Reeva had slammed the door shut and locked it because she was fleeing from Oscar who was trying to kill her during an overheated argument. Mrs. Steenkamp, Reeva's mother, believed likewise. She told a journalist: "I think it was an argument about something and she ran away. She was afraid and locked herself in the toilet. You don't normally lock the door in the company of someone you trust."

The prosecution and others may have been correct in believing Reeva was fleeing from a murderous Oscar. They would, however, have been correct in a very different sense than they thought. The element of accuracy in their theory would not necessarily mean Oscar was lying, as they insisted. Factually, he may have been trying to kill Reeva—but actually during dream-enactment in which he was convinced she was a dangerous intruder. Subjectively, he may have thought he needed to protect both himself and her by attacking trespassers. Such beliefs are commonplace in RBD. In this transient hallucinatory confusion, Oscar may have assaulted the human being who was physically closest and dearest to him, mistakenly believing she was the intruder, just like Brian Thomas and so many others have done.

This parasomnia explanation not only makes the prosecution's view correct but also renders Oscar's version accurate—albeit in very different ways than either of them realized. Prosecutor Nel's charge that Oscar tried to kill Reeva would have been *objectively* true, but would not correspond with Oscar's internal experience in which he was trying to protect his girlfriend by eliminating a dangerous intruder. Only concepts from the scientific realms of sleep, dreaming, and parasomnia can encompass both these seemingly irreconcilable, passionately held viewpoints that clashed so dramatically in the courtroom.

Not only slamming the toilet door, but also locking it, cellphone in hand, shift from being incomprehensible mysteries to being eminently understandable when considered from the perspective of parasomnia. The credibility of this sleep and dreaming disorder hypothesis for understanding these enigmas increases if we consider them not in isolation but rather in relation to all the other profoundly puzzling aspects of this case discussed earlier that also moved from incomprehensibility to comprehensibility when viewed as indicators of disordered sleep and dreaming. In each instance, these scientific concepts enabled us to fathom these conspicuous mysteries that are so essential to comprehending what might have transpired in the wee hours of that cursed Saint Valentine's Day.

Chapter 13

SOUNDS SHATTERING SILENCE

The shrewd guess, the fertile hypothesis, the courageous leap to a tentative conclusion—these are the most valuable coins of the thinker at work.
—Jerome S. Bruner,
Harvard University

To prove their theory that Oscar and Reeva had been arguing and that his temper caused him to kill her, the prosecution summoned neighbors who claimed they had heard a couple yelling that night. After listening to expert opinion as to whether people could know from which home a scream was coming, and whether it was male or female, Judge Masipa ruled that the neighbors' testimony could not be taken as credible evidence supporting the prosecution's case. Some observers agreed with the Judge; others continued to believe the neighbors. There is a third possibility: we can consider the neighbors' reports from the perspective of disordered sleep and dreaming.

Sleep screaming happens fairly often in parasomnia. This fact was well conveyed in the clever title of an article in the October 2004 issue of *Minnesota Monthly Magazine*. The piece was called *To Sleep, Perchance to Scream*.

When someone simply sits up rapidly in bed and yells, that is sleep terror. If that person jumps out of bed and runs around, out the door, or through a window, that more complex and potentially dangerous behavior would be sleep terror complicated by somnambulism.

Roger Federer, one of the world's most famous tennis players, experienced a violent episode of sleep terror compounded by somnambulism. Professor Schenck (2007) described how this elite athlete leapt out of bed, screamed, then ran and hit the corner of the bed, bruising himself. These events happened the night before his quarterfinal match in the 2006 Japan Open. Roger's fiancée attributed this odd episode to stress he was under related to playing too much tennis. Federer himself believed this parasomnia had been triggered by the 'sake bomber' he had enjoyed with his dinner. Recall Peter Buck, REM's lead guitar player, attributing his parsomniac assault to a combination of alcohol plus a sleeping pill. Might Roger, having flown to the Far East for a tennis tournament, have topped his sake bomber off with a sleeping pill?

Sleep terrors are usually associated with simple, terrifying imagery instigating yelling and/or other frenzied behavior. Whereas a person may have a long, intricately plotted nightmare leading up to a fear-associated awakening and, rarely, may cry or yell upon waking up, it takes almost no time and minimal stimuli to set off pavor nocturnus. In sleep laboratories, a soft beep from the monitor, or another patient coughing in the next room, can trigger sleep terror events in people prone to them. At home, a passing car or someone closing a door (like Reeva going to the toilet or opening the bathroom window) can trigger pavor nocturnus.

The wife of one of Professor Schenck's patients, David, always tries to be very quiet when coming to bed after her husband has fallen asleep. Nonetheless, David screams the second he hears her open the door. These hair-trigger responses to small stimuli only happen during vulnerable sleep stages.

In a chapter in *Case Studies in Sleep Neurology:*

Common and Uncommon Presentations entitled "A Terrified and Terrifying Scream, Dr. Hrayr P. Attarian described a forty-eight-year-old woman, Mrs. A, who would sit upright in bed, let out blood curdling screams, then pat the bed with both hands. She often went back to sleep without realizing what had happened. On rare occasions, she was wakened by her shouts and could report vague memories of spiders falling on the bed. These events initially occurred once or twice a month. Mrs. A had night terrors as a child. They went away spontaneously after a year. Throughout adolescence and early adulthood, pavor nocturnus only occurred rarely, when she was sleep deprived. In Professor Attarian's laboratory, after having fallen asleep, Mrs. A's eyes opened. She glanced about with a terrified look on her face and let out a short series of increasingly loud screams.

Dr. Attarian noted that night terrors consist of abrupt arousal, sudden "blood curdling" screaming, followed by incoherent vocalizations. These patients manifest intense fear, accompanied by flushing, sweating, pupillary dilation and rapid breathing. Rarely do they leave their beds. When they do, they usually jump up and run through their homes, ending the episode with sleepwalking. Attacks usually occur during the first third of the sleep but, when frequent, they can occur at any time of the night and during daytime naps.

According to the diagnostic criteria of the International Classification of Sleep Disorders-3, the necessary features to make the sleep terror diagnosis are as follows: 1) A sudden episode of terror occurs during sleep, usually beginning with a cry or loud scream accompanied by autonomic and behavioral manifestations of intense fear; 2) At least one of the following four features is present: difficulty arousing the individual; mental confusion when awakened; partial or total amnesia for the events; dangerous or potentially dangerous behaviors; 3) The disturbance is not better explained by another sleep, medical, neurological or mental disorder, or by substance abuse, or by the side effects of medication.

The etiology and pathophysiology of sleep terror remain unknown, although there is a clear familial tendency. Prevalence in prepubertal children is 1-6%, peaking around age 6. By age 8, 50% of these children no longer have attacks. Only 36% continue having them into adolescence. In adults, the prevalence drops to approximately 1%. The majority of these adults experiencedd these terrors as children and continued to have them throughout adolescence, often at a lower frequency. Breathing disorders, e.g., obstructive sleep apnea, can trigger pavor nocturnus. In those cases, treating the breathing disorder usually ends the terrors.

Professor Schenck (2007) cites a story told by Gertrude, the wife of his patient, Martin. Her account seems germane to how Reeva might have perceived Oscar's screaming at her and the imaginary intruders.

> Martin's sleep disorder started ...the month he retired. ...He would literally go wild ...throw his arms all over. ...He would do so much real loud screaming, and that was very disturbing. I'd wonder why he, why *anyone*, would scream so loud at night. Rarely was it words that you could understand—mostly it was nonsense talk. I think the screaming was the most disturbing part to me. It was violent screaming, and it would wake me out of a sound sleep. Afterward, I couldn't stop shaking for a long time.
>
> One of our daughters got divorced and was living with us for four months with her two little boys, and I remember the six-year-old would say, "Grandpa, why do you scream so much at night?" It must have been pretty traumatic for the little boys. ...
>
> He grabbed my hair one time, pulling it for all it's worth, and I woke him up to ask him what

was going on. He said, "There's a skunk in the tent. I'm getting rid of it." [*BW: This is rapid eye movement sleep behavior disorder.*] Earlier, he had gone fishing in Canada, and actually had a skunk in the tent, and he kicked it out. The scariest of all was the time he had his hands around my throat and was actually choking me. ...

It was never easy to wake him up. I could get him to stop, but it was hard to get him fully awake. He would go right back to dreaming in no time.

But he was always trying to protect me. He thought somebody was trying to get me, people trying to get in our house. [*BW: like Oscar Pistorius' conviction that he was trying to protect himself and Reeva from home invaders, and Kenneth Parks' and Brian Thomas' similar beliefs.*] He thought they were coming up the stairs, and he jumped out of bed a few times. ...

We were travelling quite a bit at that time, and the thing that concerned me was, if he did this loud screaming and we were in a motel, somebody would alert the authorities or the officials of the hotel that I was being abused. ...

He used a lot of force—that's the thing that was so scary. The other thing I worried so much about was that he did have guns for hunting. I was so afraid that he would get up and get a gun and probably shoot us. ...

I've timed him as long as thirty minutes in one dream. I can see his eyes moving back and forth during his dreams [*BW: rapid eye movement*] as long as there's enough light in the room. ...

I even asked my daughter what she remembers,

and she said the screaming would wake her up and she would be very shaken for a long time.

Professor Schenck (2005) informed one patient that waking up with a piercing scream is usual in night terrors. "With you a typical episode is having a night terror with intermittent, frightening dreams, waking up while hallucinating the dream, acting on your terror with frenzied behavior, and then taking a while to collect yourself" (p. 247). Much of that description might apply to Oscar.

Some neighbors insisted they heard a woman screaming in the Blade Runner's home well before they heard him fire the fatal bullets. Judge Masipa believed the acoustic expert who testified that it would be difficult or impossible for anyone to be sure that panicky screaming emanated from a male versus a female. It is additionally interesting to consider the difficulty discriminating gender differences in vocal qualities from the perspective of parasomnia. Professor Schenck (2005) described his patient, David, who had no sleep complaints until he injured his back at work, whereupon his administrator began a campaign to fire him. David began having dreams about people with blank eyes who followed him, hid behind stairs with knives, and pointed guns at him. Might these individuals have represented David's boss who was unable to see him (blank eyes) in any kind, compassionate, human way? In response to those nocturnal threats, David often dove off the edge of his bed, smashing into the wall as he attempted to escape. One time his upstairs neighbors heard his screaming and came to check on his wife. They believed it was her screaming because it was such a *high-pitched noise—a sound David says he ordinarily cannot make.* Clearly the difficulty witnesses can have differentiating male from female yelling can be enormously compounded in cases involving parasomnia.

Another time, David's *high-pitched screaming* caused the neighbors to call out through the heat ducts to his wife, believing she was being attacked. David awoke to find himself choking his spouse while enacting a dream of fighting off those blank-eyed attackers (rapid eye movement sleep behavior disorder).

Some of David's dream-enactments involved *awakening within a dream*. He was able to move around while dreaming about being asleep and dreaming, then waking up—within the dream. On one occasion:

> I was screaming so terribly that it woke up our upstairs neighbors and they were ready to call the police. The wife yelled through the heat vent to my wife, asking if she was alright. Melody assured them she was ok, and said it was just me having a nightmare. After I left for work they came down to make certain she was alright.
>
> I have been in real-life situations where I have been scared, but nothing compares with the fear in these dreams. ...When I start screaming, first I hear myself and what is amazing is that it is such a high pitch, two notes above middle 'C' and I ordinarily can't make sounds anywhere near that pitch. That night three weeks ago, the neighbors thought it was my wife screaming.

Professor Schenck (2007) described another sleep shouter, Mel, whose voice was completely different during parasomnia. "The tone of his voice, volume, rhythm, inflections, content, and duration of speech were radically distinct. This is a common finding with RBD." Without treatment, Schenck's statistics would predict that Mel had a 25% chance of moving on to violent dream enactment.

A married couple came to Dr. Schenck's (2005, p. 260) sleep center. The wife had a problem with nocturnal terrors. One night her screaming triggered night terror in her husband. According to their neighbors, both husband and wife were hollering in alternating fashion at the top of their lungs. She was shouting something like, 'Don't do this!' He was screaming something bizarre. The police were called because the neighbors thought this was domestic violence.

In an online comment on November 17, 2017 concerning Oscar's case, a woman shared: "You know what always get me about this case? The evidence of one of the ear witnesses who said they heard a woman screaming for help and then a man shouting "help" too. The witness said they thought the man was mocking the woman. How awful is that? Poor Reeva, desperately hiding in a toilet while her ranting, yelling, armed boyfriend mocks her desperate pleas for help. I hope he rots." This commentator might be somewhat relieved to know that in parasomnia it can be difficult to know the gender of the screamer, let alone their intent (e.g., mocking).

The fact that male screaming during RBD and pavor nocturnus with or without somnambulism can sound like a woman's voice adds a new perspective that reinforces the acoustic expert's opinion at Oscar's trial that it can be difficult to distinguish male from female shouting. Those neighbors who insisted they heard a woman screaming in the Blade Runner's home before bullets were fired might now, if open-minded about the dream and parasomnia hypotheses, be receptive to the idea that the sounds they perceived and interpreted as female screaming could have come from Oscar himself.

Chapter 14

BAD WITNESSING

History is a nightmare from which I am trying to awake.

—James Joyce, *Ulysses*

In her Judgment, Judge Masipa wrote:

> The accused was a very poor witness. While during evidence in chief he seemed composed and logical, with a result that his evidence flowed and made sense, while giving his version under cross-examination he lost his composure. Counsel for defence sought to explain the accused's poor performance on the witness stand thus: The accused was suffering from enormous emotional stress; had been traumatised by the incidents of 14 February 2013 and was under medication when he gave his evidence.
>
> This argument does not make sense in my view. I say this for the following reasons: The accused's performance during examination in chief could not be faulted. It was only under cross-examination that he contradicted himself and visibly felt uncomfortable. In any event, this

court was not appraised of the fact, that the factors mentioned above might interfere with the accused's ability to give evidence.

It does not assist to mention them now when the trial is over. It is so that most witnesses do find giving evidence an uncomfortable experience, especially when they give evidence for the first time. It follows therefore that someone in the position of the accused, would find giving evidence a harrowing experience as he re-lives the incident [BW: *especially under hostile cross-examination by a lawyer whose courtroom style had earned him the ominous nickname, "The Pitbull"*].

However, what we are dealing with here is the fact that the accused was, amongst other things, an evasive witness. In my view there are several reasons for this. He failed to listen properly to questions put to him under cross-examination, giving an impression that he was more worried by the impact that his answers might cause, rather than the questions asked.

Often a question requiring a straightforward answer turned into a point of debate about what another witness did or said. When contradictions were pointed out to him or when he was asked why certain propositions were not put to state witnesses, he often blamed his legal team for the oversight.

Continuing her Judgement, Judge Masipa noted that Reeva was killed under peculiar circumstances. There are many aspects that do not make any sense, she proclaimed. She proceeded to list her four major examples of incomprehensibility that I discussed in detail. Those profoundly puzzling elements, and the extent to which they might have contributed to a feeling that Oscar was a poor witness, are all thrown into radically new light when viewed from the perspective of parasomnia. If he had been in a state of dream enactment and confusional arousal while participating in and observing the events of February 14, 2013, one would scarcely expect him to provide a coherent narrative. In dreams of convenience, nightmares, dream-enactments, confusional arousal, and other parasomnias, gaps, contradictions, illogical reasoning, and amnesias are common.

Neuropsychologists knowledgeable of the brain's fear circuitry tell us that under conditions of severe anxiety, whatever memory traces are recorded are often fragmentary and incomplete. Our brains typically try to complete gestalts, to fill the gaps in and between whatever fragments they have access to. We are hardwired to try to bridge breaches in understanding in order to situate ourselves in worlds that make sense. We saw an example of this narrative construction process with Kenneth Parks. He concocted a story in which he was sure someone had drugged him, dragged him to his car, and driven him to his in-laws' residence. In their home he believed he must have slowly come to his senses, whereupon he saw his kidnapper attempting to kill his in-laws, prompting Ken to spring into action, slicing his hands severely in the process. Wild and impossible though this story surely was, for Ken it made sense out of what would otherwise have been a more disturbingly incomprehensible, fragmented experience.

Even Kenneth's wildly improbable tale makes some metaphoric sense if we consider that parts of it may have reflected his subjective reality. He had been extremely stressed and sleep deprived for days. He was therefore, in a sense, 'drugged,' that is, in an altered neurochemical state. (Sleep deprived subjects perform like intoxicated people on performance tests even though they may believe they are performing very well.) In this 'drugged state,' Ken may have fallen into deep sleep conducive to somnambulism. He was then 'driven' to his in-laws, not by some intruder who slipped a soporific into his Kool-Aid but, rather, by unconscious forces, perhaps pertaining to shame, terror, and rage that he might have been experiencing in relation to his imminent confessions to his in-laws and grandparents.

At his in-laws', Ken came unstably to his senses. It would be accurate for him to say that at that moment, metaphorically, a 'stranger' (i.e., a version of himself unknown to himself) was assaulting his in-laws. Repeatedly in dream enactments one encounters that same scenario: a wild animal or malevolent intruder assaults loved ones and the dreamer tries to protect them aggressively. Ken's alien attacker would have been an estranged part of himself—"the stranger within." Carl Jung referred to this mysterious being as The Shadow—an archetype we all possess. Sometimes this Shadow possesses us.

At the level of subjective reality, the idea of Kenneth struggling with a murderous stranger reflects the conflict he would have had between any wish to attack his in-laws versus his determination to never do them any harm. Even a story as bizarre as Ken's begins to make some sense when viewed as his metaphoric attempt to understand otherwise incomprehensible, fragmentary, elusive events apprehended in a state of altered consciousness.

In June 2016, shortly before his second sentencing, Oscar participated in an interview with British television network, ITV. With aching voice, he stated: "I understand the pain that people feel that loved her and miss her. I feel that same pain. I feel that same hate for myself. I feel that same difficulty in understanding this. I look back and I think, I always think, 'How did this possibly happen? How could this have happened?' " Despite the fact that he had offered to the Court and the world a generally rational story of what had transpired that awful night, he seemed to know that this account did not fully explain what had occurred. "How could this have happened?", he continued to ask. Notwithstanding the fact that his story was infinitely more believable than Kenneth Parks', nonetheless Oscar sensed it could not fully account for all that happened that night. For that longed for, more complete and convincing narrative, a more knowledgeable, reliable witness than himself was required. That is where the expert testimony provided by this book is necessary to supplement and transform those aspects of Oscar's account that were missing, poor, paradoxical, contradictory, and unbelievable into a more coherent, plausible view of what actually transpired.

Chapter 15

MAGICAL MYSTERY TOUR

Fortunately, somewhere between chance and mystery lies imagination, the only thing that protects our freedom, despite the fact that people keep trying to reduce it or kill it off altogether.

—Luis Buñuel

Previous chapters focussed on psychological and legal matters crucial for understanding the shocking events that occurred in Oscar Pistorius' home on Saint Valentine's Day 2013. Discussion adhered closely to the facts, and to gaping holes—mysterious antimatter in the fabric of those reported occurrences. Relevant ideas pertaining to dreams, parasomnias, and non-insane automatism were introduced. Might knowing more about the fascinating nature of dreaming, the structure of the mind, the dynamic (repressed) unconscious, and other such intriguing matters help shed even more light on the enigmatic phenomena we are exploring?

Prior to venturing into these more theoretically informed, speculative domains, a word of warning. Parts of this chapter may not appeal to those who prefer sticking to the facts. They may not want to struggle with these more challenging ideas. These readers need not worry. Subsequent chapters will not depend on these more imaginative ideas.

The rest of this book will be as grounded and comprehensible as, hopefully, the preceding chapters have been.

In *The Interpretation of Dreams*, Freud described two principles of mental functioning. He referred to the rational reasoning of everyday life as *secondary process* cognition. In contrast, the unconscious operates in accord with different, *primary process* principles. Immersing himself in the world of dreams where primary process rules, Freud asserted that their study constitutes the royal road to understanding unconscious processes.

Expanding on Freud's seminal ideas, Melanie Klein posited two other forms of psychological organization. At the beginning of life, we operate predominantly in the Paranoid-Schizoid (PS) Position. Schizoid means split. The infant's worldview is divided into one that feels *good* versus another that feels *bad* (persecutory, 'paranoid'). To capture the primitive, sensual, body-based nature of these diametrically different domains, Klein labeled the perceived 'objects' characterizing these states as the *Good* and *Bad Breast*. Her American contemporary, Harry Stack Sullivan, spoke of these dissociated infantile realms of the good and bad mother as being linked to *good me, bad me* (and *not-me*).

In Klein's view, the infantile mind cannot encompass contradictions and nuance. Things are experienced in black or white terms (all good or all bad). Absence of the beloved mother is not viewed as a temporary frustration. Her departure for more than a brief time feels catastrophic. The vacuum created by her unavailability is quickly filled by the persecutory object. When infants feel frustration, agony, and terror, they are likely to feel this malevolent mother is intentionally inflicting these affects on them. When these children acquire language, they tell us about dreadful descendants of this bad breast (evil witches, dangerous monsters under the bed).

It is only with maturation that we become able to construct a more complex view of our mothers and the world. Klein called that more evolved state the Depressive (D) Position. American psychoanalyst Thomas Ogden suggested renaming it the Historical Position to indicate that in it one no longer lives in dissociated moments of now. Instead, one dwells in a present connected to a past and a future. While studying at the Toronto Institute for Contemporary Psychoanalysis, Brian Shelley suggested calling this the Ambivalent Position. His term captures the individual's new, important ability to have mixed feelings about someone. In a closely related spirit, American psychoanalyst Jessica Benjamin referred to the Bivalent Position. All these contributors point to significant features we acquire as we advance beyond the Paranoid-Schizoid domain.

A mother shared with me that as she tried to comfort her young son while he was suffering from an ear infection, he plaintively asked, "Momma, why are you hurting my ear?" Feeling she was the cause of his suffering, he seemed to have at least one foot in PS. This boy was using his still generally trusting image of his mother to try to reconcile emotionally conflicting perceptions of her (good breast, bad breast) in an attempt to shift the balance between PS and D in a more favorable direction.

On Saint Valentine's Day 2013, during his dream of inconvenience, Oscar may not only have heard a noise in the bathroom but may also, in a state of light sleep, have unconsciously sensed Reeva was not in his bed. He may have been unable to simply dream that inference away to continue slumbering. Her absence might have resonated with early developmental abandonment terrors, precipitating a slide into PS territory. At that point, in his vivid words: "I felt a sense of terror rushing over me." Good Breast Reeva was gone. (Baby) Oscar was now dangerously alone or, more precisely, in the unbidden company of the Bad Breast (aka the malevolent intruder).

In relation to Oscar's descent into the paranoid-schizoid realm, recall Professor Schenck's patient's description of "instant nightmares" that interrupt his normal dreaming, signaling the onset of rapid eye movement sleep behavior disorder. Suddenly machine guns would emerge from the wall and shoot at this man. These terrifying, precipitous shifts suggest the abrupt disappearance of the ambience of the good breast and its immediate replacement by the persecutory, murderous mammary.

Similar to what Professor Schenck's patient experienced, a patient of mine who was endeavoring to find and heal the roots of her difficulties said: "My mother's words felt like a machine gun ... like a barrage of bullets coming right at me. There was no one to protect me. I was completely alone. I couldn't trust my own mother to love me." She recalled a time when she herself had gone "ballistic, insane" with her daughter. Fortunately her husband was there to calm her down. My patient continued: "My mother always had her finger on the button. She could torpedo my life at any moment." This imagery seemed like a reference to the current rhetorical battle between U.S. President Donald Trump and North Korean leader, Kim Jong Un, as they threatened to press their nuclear buttons, launching missiles to annihilate each other, their societies, and perhaps the entire world. "There was no defense against mother's anger. How can you trust anyone if you can't trust your mother? ... Fear of mother's anger nearly killed me. I tried to appease her. I never felt the world was safe because any connection to mother never lasted."

In Oscar's comparable "instant nightmare," emergency situation, he might be expected to unconsciously deploy active *splitting*. This defense, characteristic of the Paranoid-Schizoid Position, involves vigorous efforts to keep good and bad separate in order to preserve the good and render our experience of the world clearer, simpler, more manageable. In this way, despite sliding into PS territory, Oscar may have hung onto some sense of the continuing existence of good Reeva (benevolent breast) beside him, securely sequestered under their cozy duvet (denial). The defensively dissociated, abandoning, persecutory aspect of Reeva (deriving its power from infantile experience) was 'safely' projected, therefore contained, albeit unstably, down the hall in the bathroom (like the monsters that children are sure are lurking in their closets). With this splitting of benevolence and malevolence, Oscar could proceed to obliterate the dangerous object in the toilet chamber, which would result in his being happily reunited with his good object.

Here again I emphasize that many of the ideas I am presenting in this chapter are purely speculative. They are intended to provide imaginative counterpoint to the very grounded inferential process that characterized the previous chapters. Hopefully most readers will find these ideas more stimulating than confusing.

"Kill or be killed" is a characteristic theme in Paranoid Schizoid states. Morality, based on concern with not harming others, does not appear until the Depressive Position becomes more dominant. Consequently, in a PS frame of mind, one cannot think of more sophisticated courses of action, such as firing warning shots. Instead, one quickly blasts multiple shots to make sure one has annihilated the bad breast.

In America, rapid fire assault weaponry, like the AR-15 and the AK-47, are the guns of choice for this endeavor. Instead of helplessly experiencing "instant nightmares" like Dr. Schenck's patient in which machine guns suddenly come out of the walls and shoot at one, one instead becomes the powerful aggressor wielding the assault rifle and becoming someone else's nightmare.

A man murdered his mother and sister, then climbed a tower at an American university. He proceeded to open fire on people below. Nightmarish phantasy and defenses had hijacked his thought processes. He needed to annihilate manifold incarnations of the bad breast (virtually everyone) to avoid the alternative scenario in which he would be the one obliterated. Lest anyone think such phantasies are exclusively experienced by the severely mentally deranged, think of how normal children play out this phantasy in their videogames as they blast powerful assault rifles at endless streams of malevolent intruders in their zombie apocalypse worlds. These phantasies are common. In the best of circumstances, they are confined to play and other imaginary realms.

Another American man experienced conflict with his mother-in-law. She was becoming bad breast. On November 5, 2017 he (and his image of her) went over the edge. He blasted his way into the church she usually attended in the small town of Sutherland, Texas. He killed half the congregation. From his tenuous foothold in reality, he had slipped into the Paranoid-Schizoid Position. It turned out that his mother-in-law was not at church that day. What to us were innocent people had, for him, evidently been contaminated by association with her. They were now bad objects, just like her. They had to be obliterated. One could say that he was the zombie in this apocalyptic scenario. From his perspective, however, he was more like the beleaguered hero eliminating malevolent zombies.

Oscar's Childhood

Apart from the fact that no one begins, or makes it through the life cycle, without encountering some nightmarish anxieties, is there any evidence that the Blade Runner may have suffered any particularly awful experiences during early developmental periods that might have provided more than usual ingredients for paranoid-schizoid experience?

Most of the world met Oscar when he was already a dashingly handsome superstar. Things had not always been so sweet. Prior to his first birthday, his little legs were amputated below his knees. One can imagine that this major surgery involved pain, separations from mother and all that was safe, secure, and familiar, and frightening interventions by strangers (intruders). Born in 1986, Oscar may have been fortunate enough to have anaesthetics during his bilateral amputations. It was only in the 1980s that these substances became a regular part of paediatric surgery. Before then, we merely gave infants drugs to paralyze their muscles so they could not squirm and scream while being operated upon. We comforted ourselves sometimes with the delusional idea that babies cannot experience pain. (We see traces of this fantasy in the soothing idea that lobsters do not feel any discomfort when we toss them into pots of boiling water.) A medical colleague shared with me the horror he experienced as a surgical resident in that era. On a particularly memorable occasion, he observed a senior colleague conducting major surgery on a premature infant, without anaesthesia. My friend will never forget what he witnessed that day.

For the infantile mind—really for any mind—such assaults on the paralyzed body represent the malicious activities of Klein's bad breast. Recall the patient with pavor nocturnus who used to wake up screaming about spiders descending into her bed. These eight-legged creatures are known for their ability to paralyze prey, preserving them to eat alive later. That woman's terrifying arachnids are akin to the machineguns that would suddenly burst out of walls, blasting Professor Schenck's patient. Klein's bad breast manifests in many forms.

Besides birth defects, amputations, separations, physical challenges, and ongoing pain, might there have been any other issues that could have contributed grist to Oscar's Paranoid-Schizoid mill? When he was just six years old, his parents divorced. Prior to that event, home life would have been contaminated by their loudly or silently berating and avoiding each other (e.g., for not being 'good breasts,' that is, for being sources of frustration rather than gratification). When they progressed from emotional tension and estrangement to actual physical separation, young Oscar experienced a further significant loss: his father relocated to a new home seven hundred miles away. When altered economic circumstances required his mother to go to work, that necessity resulted in a sort of double parenting loss.

In the rougher neighborhood to which Mrs. Pistorius and her children moved, they experienced several break-ins. Constantly anticipating the next intruders, she slept with a loaded pistol under her pillow. When Oscar grew up, he adopted a similar practice.

When Mrs. Pistorius heard sounds in the night, she often jumped up in bed, phoned the police, then woke her children. Hustling them to her bedroom, she would lock the door and wait for the police to arrive. Her idea that the slightest sound could signify imminent disaster against which one needed to be armed and prepared to act decisively was instilled in Oscar at a very young age.

In these ways, anticipated robberies in the Blade Runner's adult life would likely have resonated with developmentally earlier experiences with home invasions, real or imagined, and with even earlier 'bad breast' experiences.

Eight years after his parents' divorce, when Oscar was fifteen, his mother remarried. What was supposed to be the beginning of a new era of greater happiness turned out otherwise. Just one month after her wedding, Sheila Pistorius had her final encounter with the bad breast in the form of terminal illness, possibly related to years of excessive alcohol consumption. At age 44, in a coma, with tubes riddling her degenerating body, Sheila could not recognize her family.

Adolescent Oscar was devastated. The author, John Carlin, reported that the teenager "lost part of himself." (Previously he literally lost part of himself in the form of bilateral amputations.) Oscar was "for all practical purposes an orphan." The Blade Runner had the dates of his mother's birth and death (May 8, 1958 and March 6, 2002) tattooed in Roman numerals on the inside of his right arm. This body modification provided a concrete, fleshy way of holding on to the disappearing good breast.

Oscar idealized his mother. She was the driving force in his life. Lacking a strong paternal presence, he may have clung to this perfect image of her to offset father absence. Beneath this idealization, Mrs. Pistorius had problems, e.g., alcohol or, more correctly, the demons this derivative of the good breast is called upon to anesthetize. Drinking herself to sleep, she often failed to awaken when her younger children, Aimée and Oscar, cried out to her.

When Reeva did not respond to Oscar's shouting to her on Saint Valentine's Day, her non-responsiveness may have been not very noteworthy to him, given his childhood experiences with an often unresponsive mother. Simultaneously, Reeva's silence may have been very noteworthy, for the very same reason. His anger and use of denial and action-oriented defenses for overlooking and plowing through such emotional absence may have been well honed during his childhood experiences with an ofttimes unwakable mother.

While Mrs. Pistorius' failure to wake up to the cries of her children may simply have been due to intoxication, those scenes also reminded me of a case of severe morning *sleep inertia* described by Professor Schenck (2007). That woman's children would run around their home writing with permanent marker pens on the walls, carpet, tub, toilet, each other, and on her. She slept soundly through all that chaos. Reflecting on those turbulent years, she recalled, "They'd jump on my bed, cry, yell, beg me to get up and feed them." These children were desperately trying to bring their mother back to life.

Trying to create a laboratory model that might enable them to explore the effects of maternal depression on young children, developmental psychologists conducted 'still face' experiments in which they instructed mothers to become immobile. This abrupt change to inanimacy is very disturbing to youngsters. Its impact resembles what French psychoanalyst André Green wrote about in "*The Dead Mother.*" In that article, he was referring to how children experience not deceased parents but, rather, emotionally unavailable, preoccupied, frequently depressed caregivers.

British pediatrician-psychoanalyst Donald Winnicott wrote similarly that when a mother is away for x minutes, her baby becomes stressed. When she is away for $x + y$ units of time, strain becomes extreme. The situation is still reparable if she returns and can comfort her child. If she is absent for $x + y + z$ time units, the damage is irreparable. Primitive defensive operations may cover the catastrophe, but it continues to take a heavy toll. "I just like to drink." "Drugs make me feel good." "Risk-taking makes me feel alive." "I can never get enough sex." "Happiness is a warm gun" (The Beatles).

Anyone who has observed toddlers knows they are typically so attached to their mothers that they cannot even allow them to go to the bathroom alone. If a mother leaves to go to the washroom, her toddler, who may have been happily occupied with other matters, usually knows their 'primary object' has stood up. The youngster's inner watchman detects mother's slightest motion and sounds the alarm. To prevent unbearable absence $(x + y)$, the child follows mama. A young mother, Erika, recently shared with me that she can hardly wait for her toddlers to grow up so she can resume going to the toilet by herself. Unlike for preschoolers, for adults being alone can sometimes be divine, not deadly.

Analogous to how toddlers monitor the whereabouts, actions, and intentions of people most important to them, while Oscar was weaving his dream of convenience to manage fan sounds catching his attention, he may have subliminally detected that Reeva had left the bed. Hearing noise emanating from the bathroom, "A sense of terror rushed over me." Catapulted into emergency mode, the Fastest Man On No Legs grabbed his gun. His lover's absence may have triggered ancient separation (annihilation) anxiety $(x + y)$. His impulsive action might be seen as an aggressivized version of how 'abandoned' toddlers spring into hot pursuit of their mothers who simply want to go to the toilet.

Edgar

Like Oscar, my five-year-old patient, Edgar, began life in difficult circumstances in Ann Arbor, Michigan. During his first year, his mother's serious medical difficulties required her to be hospitalized. Like Oscar's mom, Edgar's had lots of anxiety. She believes her preoccupation with possibly dying impeded early bonding with her son. After that trying year, however, she was in love with him. "All's well that ends well," one would like to think, but life is not always so simple.

When Edgar was four, his parents adopted a baby girl, Sue-Yin, from China. Three years later, I met Edgar. For a few years, he had been manifesting oppositional defiant behaviors. He never seemed satisfied, his mother reported. His social relationships were suffering.

During Edgar's first year, his mother had been physically and/or emotionally absent for at least the distressing $x + y$ units of time that Winnicott described. She may have been gone for the catastrophic $x + y + z$. Troubling effects from postpartum separation seemed to reverberate in Edgar's psyche for years. Rather than experiencing crippling anxiety, thanks to primitive self-protective mechanisms (denial, manic grandiosity, projective identification), he became a master at causing others to feel anxious, angry, frantic, and unhappy. He developed an *externalizing* disorder (as opposed to *internalizing* disorders like anxiety or depression), forcing others to experience the anxiety and misery he could not tolerate. It would be challenging to help Edgar believe it might be okay to relax his self-protective character armor, enabling him to find his way back onto a healthier, more harmonious developmental track.

At our first appointment, when his mother was leaving with Sue-Yin, Edgar requested she bring back some of his favorite chocolates. He repeated this entreaty every session. Her absence could be tolerable if he could believe she was still connected to him, thinking about his needs.

Seemingly in order to express how hungrily upset these separations made him feel, Edgar announced that tyrannosaurus rex (from my toy collection) was going to eat a winged robot. Perhaps this flying creature embodied the 'unfeeling' way Edgar's mother took flight and 'abandoned' him, especially when he was a baby, triggering impulses to devour her in order to avoid feeling empty (Freud's oral stage). Via this global incorporative act, he could keep mama inside him forever. The winged robot vigorously tried to escape but T-Rex persisted in pursuing him. The dinosaur was powerful (manic grandiosity) and angry. Far from being fearful, he stimulated terror in others, probably even in a strong robot.

Edgar's violent fantasy shifted to a baby doll. When I asked why this infant was being attacked, he explained: "Because she is ugly and poohs in public." I imagined this hated infant might represent Sue-Yin. At a deeper level, this despised image could stand for Edgar himself, containing his explanation of why his mother abandoned him during his first year (for being messy, smelly, unattractive, unlovable).

Edgar's attention shifted from this baby doll to a picture of a girl holding a trophy in the board game, Snakes & Ladders. She must be killed because she is ugly, he proclaimed. Moving back to the baby doll, Edgar had soldiers shoot that infant. A woman appeared and knocked the military men down. This maternal figure may have represented Edgar's mother, and the side of him that wanted to stand up for Sue-Yin insofar as she represented not only an unwanted, ambivalently regarded younger sibling but also his own unlovable/lovable self that had, long ago, been 'abandoned' by his own mother.

Edgar announced his intention to put the baby in jail—a far less extreme fate. This advance to mere confinement represents a move away from the earliest terrors and violence of the paranoid-schizoid position toward the less extreme anxieties characterizing the more evolved, depressive position. In the language of Freud and his colleague, Karl Abraham, this change reflects the crucial psychosexual progression from anal expulsion (the deadly blast of bullets from the soldier's rifles) to anal retention (imprisonment).

Edgar ended up jailing the woman instead of the baby. Perhaps this turn of events expressed that it was really the comings and going of his mother that he wanted to control. As the play proceeded, he usually referred to this woman as a baby, possibly alluding to the close identification of mother and daughter, and also to blurry boundaries between him and his mama rooted in his earliest years. In that era (and continuing) his baby self needed to find some way to hold onto his mother (to imprison her). He needed to retain her in a jail of his own making rather than permitting her to go far away (e.g., to be hospitalized).

We often tell children they are going to love having a new sibling. Our offspring often obligingly concur with this merry sentiment. Usually they also have very different feelings about this changing, challenging situation. Edgar loved Sue-Yin but, in order to not feel and reveal more than this socially approved emotion, he probably felt the need to repress sibling rivalry, particularly anal expulsive, murderous impulses. Recall my adolescent patient, Paul, and the horror and panic he experienced when his destructive feelings toward his younger sister, Paula, emerged in a dream. So abhorrent was this image of slicing his sibling's throat that Paul fled treatment, even though he had found our work helpful and promising. It was only many months later, when his flight from his inner world crashed, that he reluctantly returned.

Edgar concluded that first therapy session by composing a book, *The Haunted House*. His title may have indicated his subliminal awareness of a need to encounter ghosts from his past if he hoped to get his psychological home in order. In this creepy dwelling, Bob and Billie disconnected booby trap lasers (bad breasts) in their basement, enabling them to open a cage. Inside that enclosure, they discovered a treasure (the good breast? his innocent, loving, pretraumatic self?). Disconnecting the booby traps may also have been Edgar's way of dissociating himself from explosive, murderous impulses toward his sister, mother, and anyone else representing them, permitting him to "treasure" them, and for them to cherish this safe, purified version of him.

Edgar was very bright. He was able to function at a highly creative, symbolic level, utilizing play and story composition to express and conceal complicated, conflicted concerns. These valuable assets were not always available to him. For example, he always found it impossible to leave when our time was up. Instead, he clung tenaciously to objects, like my stopwatch or a ream of paper – items he found in his determined search of my premises. He adamantly refused to part unless he could take the object of his desire with him. He longed to keep these 'treasures' in his psychic home. "Those friends thou hast, and their adoption tried, grapple them to thy soul with hoops of steel" (Shakespeare, *Hamlet*). For Edgar, these symbols of the good breast would radiate their loving, protective presence throughout our weeklong separation, counteracting the bad breast ghosts that haunted his inner world. It took considerable persuasion before Edgar could let go of these things. Ultimately he would concur with the proposition that reunion with the cherished *objet du jour* (and me) would happen soon enough. He could then leave with his mother and Sue-Yin.

With respect to his mother's initial complaint, one might say it was not exactly the case that Edgar was "never satisfied." Rather it was very challenging to help him to move from terrified, angry dissatisfaction (related to separation) to feeling adequate safety, security, and contentment (that is, to shift from $x + y$ to x or better).

In our fifth session, as Edgar's mother and sister were leaving, he again asked his mom to bring back chocolates. By now, both he and I knew it was highly unlikely this wish would be gratified, for it had been consistently frustrated after all previous appointments. Edgar picked up my stapler (a tool designed for connecting objects) and flung it to the ground. "It's stupid!" Knowing he liked that machine and had used it appropriately in previous projects, I asked what was so dumb about it. "It doesn't do what I want," he quipped.

Although I had not noticed that handy instrument being obstreperous, Edgar's angry description seemed like it might have fit his feelings about his mother departing and, making matters even worse, never bringing back chocolates. His violence toward the stapler might reflect *displacement* of his anger at his mother onto the 'safer' inanimate tool. He may also have been deploying *projective identification* to put that bad part of him that he felt his mother thought was stupid and unlovable into the stapler.

The last time I saw Edgar before the summer break, he had a bad guy kill an elephant. Seconds later, the murderer crashed into a wall, then tumbled off a tower to his death. Via displacement, the pachyderm may have become the object of Edgar's hostile feelings toward his abandoning, bad breast mother, and perhaps toward me in a manifestation of negative maternal transference (sentiments displaced from a parent figure, often of long ago onto, the therapist). In that latter role, I was the supposedly nice, helpful, psychotherapist who, much to Edgar's dislike, cruelly ends sessions when it suits me, not even attempting to assuage the hurt inflicted by at least providing valuable parting presents (presence) – not chocolates, but stopwatches, reams of paper, ten dollar bills, etc. To top off my negligence, I was now 'abandoning' Edgar for the entire summer (even though it was him and his family, not me, leaving town for a nice vacation in Michigan's Upper Peninsula).

In keeping with the more civilized side of Edgar's personality (ego, superego), his annihilating, bad guy self (id) had to be disowned, judged, found guilty, and punished. Accordingly, the malevolent figure in his pachyderm play was dropped from the tower. Unacceptable aggression must be obliterated or at least repressed (jailed). Any unauthorized breakouts from psychic prison must be responded to by superego retribution. Fortunately, Edgar was able to channel these intense feelings into 'play.'

From Edgar to Oscar

As adults, Oscar Pistorius and his younger sister, Aimée, seemed to have a close, loving relationship. Long ago, like Edgar, Oscar might have had some very different feelings about the unsolicited arrival of baby Aimée. Mother's diversion of some of her limited attention to her newest child might have constituted an unwelcome loss for young Oscar. One might call this felt deprivation an attention deficit disorder. This offensive dispersal of maternal solicitude could be expected to trigger anxiety, anger, and increased activity in the Blade-Runner-to-be—as primary reactions, protests, and defenses against this disequilibrating, threatening change to the status quo.

As Oscar matured, his love of Aimée no doubt grew. She and his mother may have become beloved models for his enthusiastic quest for ideal romantic love—most recently found with Reeva. Just as Edgar defensively displaced his rage at his departing mother onto the baby doll, elephant, winged robot, woman, and stupid stapler, Oscar may have shifted similar separation anxiety and rage in relation to his mother and his new love, Reeva, onto the imaginary burglars who, he was sure, had, like baby Aimée, invaded his home. In his psychic reality, derived from his developmental history, there was always some sort of dangerous love robbery ongoing, or about to happen, in his haunted mental house. These feared burglaries may have related to archaic 'thefts' he had experienced (e.g., with his mother in relation to his father, his mother in relation to Aimée, his father's leaving, his alcoholic mother's unavailability, etc.). *Et tu, Reeva!*

Lovers in Loos

"I shat my lover in the loo! I shat my lover in the loo!" So cried a schizophrenic girl, repeatedly, aboard an evacuation train prior to World War Two. Psychoanalyst Hanna Segal happened to be riding that same public conveyance. She believed the girl was, in phantasy, reversing her terrifying separation situation. Unconsciously, the girl wanted to feel she was the one initiating the evacuation, the terrifying loss, that felt as final as being flushed down the toilet or murdered. It feels better to be the powerful shooter than the helpless entity being killed, be it in a zombie apocalypse or a Nazi holocaust. It is preferable to be the shitter than the shit—the left behind, flushed away, devalued object. Such explosive fantasies involve denial, turning passive into active, transforming impotence into omnipotence, and projective identification (placing an intolerable self-state into someone or something else).

At a deep level, Oscar may have been struggling with an unconscious phantasy pertaining to feared separation similar to that girl on the train. Acting out terror and rage, he, too, shat his lover in the loo. Like the girl, he also proclaimed what he had done to those around him. As with the train passengers, his audience similarly served as witnesses to his overwhelming grief and guilt.

In her recent book, *Reeva: A Mother's Story*, Mrs. Steenkamp shared her knowledge, or belief, of some facts that, if true, would lead us to think that Oscar may have been attempting to manage heightened separation anxiety at the time he killed his girlfriend. "Her clothes were packed. There is no doubt in our minds: she had decided to leave Oscar that night." Even if this imminent departure were only a remote possibility, Oscar's unconscious mind would have had a major destabilizing fear to grapple with when he relaxed his vigilance to fall asleep on the eve of Saint Valentine's Day 2013.

Sleep disorder expert Rosalind Cartwright discussed a case where the prosecution challenged a *sleepshooting* defense on the grounds that the man had a history of abusing his wife and children. As a result, his spouse intended to leave. The prosecutor produced an undated note police discovered in the deceased's handbag. It described her plan to depart with the children after Christmas. The woman was murdered on December 26. Dr. Cartwright considered this killing was likely the result of violent parasomnia. The man had not benefitted from an adequate defense based on scientific evidence. Professor Cartwright is probably correct. In addition to whatever neurophysiological, parasomniac vulnerabilities this man may have had, I wonder whether this husband, sensing his wife might leave, may have harbored anxiety and hostility toward her that played a role in his violence. The fact that his previous habit of abuse escalated to murder on or around the very time she was planning to abandon him makes this possibility plausible.

Professor Cartwright cites another case where a woman with a five-year history of non-REM parasomnia (sleepwalking, sleepdriving) dozed off one evening around 10 p.m. after watching a horror movie. She awoke at 6 a.m. to find her hands covered in blood. On the kitchen cutting board there was more blood. Next to the trashcan she found the remains of her cat. Alarmed, she booked an appointment with Dr. Cartwright. This lady was found to have severe obstructive sleep apnea (OSA). This condition was eliminated by a continuous positive airway pressure (CPAP) ventilator, a device that applies mild air pressure to keep the breathing pathways open while the patient sleeps. This treatment rendered her free of all her OSA related parasomnias.

It seems possible that the atmosphere, activities, relationship patterns, and spirit of the horror movie that this woman had been watching managed to be picked up by her unconscious. (Recall Kenneth Parks, prior to his killing spree, falling asleep after watching an episode of *Saturday Night*

Live in which there were several violent incidents.) Some of these cinematic elements may have influenced her dreaming. Due to nonREM parasomnia related to OSA, her dream life spilled into reality, resulting in her butchering her beloved pet.

As we witnessed with Edgar and the girl on the evacuation train, fear of abandonment can trigger primitive terrors, murderous rage, and extreme defenses. All too many men have killed girlfriends or wives in order to establish at least a delusion of control when they feared abandonment. Many people think of these assassins as 'fucking bastards.' That vulgar description may not be inappropriate at one level. At a deeper level, they are actually terrified, enraged *infants*. Unconsciously they may feel like they were, and still are unwanted babies (bastards). They were never able to learn to understand and manage their feelings about separation and loss in ways that would permit them to transcend trauma and emotionally grow up in a cohesive manner conducive to healthy psychological functioning and relationships. To magically protect themselves from their separation terror, they desperately forge what feels to be the only possible safe identity, that of the powerful, frightening, dispenser of death. "I am not afraid of separation and obliteration. I make others suffer those fears and fates."

For healthier men, these early anxieties, and defenses, being of lesser intensity, can be kept safely in the unconscious. Even some of these males may go to extreme lengths to keep their fears unknown. Recall how terrified my adolescent patient, Paul, was when his murderous rage at his younger sister emerged into consciousness in a discombobulating nightmare in which he slit her throat. Unable to contemplate such a self-state, even in a dream, even while in therapy, he had to flee from it, and from the helpful treatment that it had contaminated. In contrast, Edgar was able to use psychotherapy to contemplate venturing into the unconscious realm (the basement of the Haunted

House) in which he had buried his intolerable emotions in order to, with the help of his friend, render archaic fears less overwhelming (disconnecting the booby traps).

Isn't Psychoanalysis about the Oedipus Complex where Breasts are primarily Attractive Secondary Sexual Characteristics rather than Primal Beings?

So far in this speculative chapter I have been imagining Oscar's situation in terms of early separation anxiety such as that which toddlers begin to experience when their mothers try to leave them to attend to their own bathroom necessities. Freud focused on later, Oedipal anxieties that he believed manifested most strongly from approximately three to five years of age (perhaps more than coincidentally the greatest time for sleep terrors). What happens if we consider Oscar's situation through the lens of these oedipal impulses, fantasies, anxieties, and defenses?

First, what is the oedipal complex? It is, in a word, complex. An (over)simplified rendering of it would be as follows: Children sense their parents have a special, intense, physical, romantic bond with each other from which youngsters feel excluded. This scenario could be seen as an advanced relational (triangular) variant on the simpler (dyadic) feeling of being unfairly excluded when mother wants to go somewhere by herself (e.g., to the toilet). Wanting to transform this crummy, frustrating oedipal situation where "two's a company, three's a crowd," children crave an exclusive relationship with at least one parent. They regard the other adult (or sometimes a sibling) as a rival whom they want to displace (eliminate). Let that other person be the excluded one. For these competitive, sometimes hostile impulses, children fear equally violent retaliation (e.g., genital damage).

The human imaginative capacity may be significantly grounded in primal scene fantasies, that is, in children's perception or imagination about parents' sexual lives, British psychoanalyst Ronald Britton stated. An imaginary room comes into existence developmentally when it becomes possible to believe that the primary object (mother) continues to exist despite her perceptual absence. Although she sometimes cannot be seen, she is now felt to continue existing in the child's image-ination. The previous ruling principle was that when good mother is out of sight, she is out of existence, rapidly replaced by the bad breast. This axiom yields to the blessed realization that mother does not completely, precipitously disappear, forever. The other room of the imagination becomes the place where she continues to spend her invisible existence, Britton wrote.

In what might be seen as a perverse enactment of the above scenario, the Argentinian military junta made many mothers and fathers disappear forever. Confining and murdering political dissidents was common in that time and place. Dropping those with differing (leftwing) political views from planes and helicopters into the ocean became a favorite pastime of the extreme rightwing rulers. The traumatic loss that these politicos themselves may have feared in their kill or be killed universe was reassuringly visited onto 'the disappeared' and their children and other loved ones. With these disobedient parents out of the way, politically correct families, hungry to enlarge their nuclear units, could now adopt these orphaned youngsters.

In Ronald Britton's framework, children's increasing understanding of the world, particularly the nature of intimate others, especially their continuing, out of sight existence, helps modulate separation anxiety, furnishing much needed security. Missing mothers are inevitably conceived of as relating to someone else, for intimate relationships are understood as a basic condition of existence. Typically that other impressive being with whom she is engaged is the father. From this point of view, the other room is the location of the primal scene. The important gain in security from knowing mother continues to be alive and well comes with some cost: feelings of exclusion, jealousy, anxiety, and anger. From this particular oedipal perspective Oscar, in a dreamy, middle of the night state of mind, hearing strange goings on in his bathroom, might have unconsciously calculated that Reeva's subliminally registered absence from his bed meant she (as heir to his mother's amazingness, and disloyalty) was messing around sexually in the other room with someone who had intruded into his longed for, exclusive romantic relationship with her. That's what always transpires in the 'other room.' Slipping in his dream into an 'instant nightmare' of concrete, primary process, paranoid-schizoid thinking, this feared betrayal could immediately become a fact. In PS, one simply knows things, with certainty, rather than as probabilities to be estimated and evaluated, as can happen when the Depressive Position holds sway. At this primitive level of cognitive functioning, the compelling fact might simply be a sense of a dangerous intrusion into his safety and security that demanded rapid response. In this moment, the 'bad object' he needed to eliminate would be what Melanie Klein referred to as the 'combined parental couple.' He could not let them (it) rob him of the sexually blissful, loving future he had in mind. They (it) needed to be obliterated. Any such thought processes would, of course, have been unconscious.

In a similar, real life scenario, recall the case of Brian Thomas. Dreaming a youth had intruded into the camper in which he and his wife were sleeping, Brian saw that young man atop his wife. Enraged, he seized this home invader by the neck and pulled him off. When Brian finally woke up, he realized he had strangled his wife to death. In a paranoid-schizoid rendering of the oedipal complex, he may have killed two birds with one stone. At a deeply repressed level, he may have felt his oedipal parents, whose intimacy excluded and threatened him, deserved capital punishment.

Of course when Brian returned to his predominant, mature, civilized self, he was devastated. Having a well-developed superego, he was prepared to face whatever punishment the judicial system determined he deserved. He immediately called the police, just like Kenneth Parks and Oscar did.

In keeping with this speculation about Oscar interpreting Reeva's absence in terms of old oedipal templates, he imagined there could have been more than one person in the small bathroom stall: "I screamed words to the effect for *him/them* to get out of my house. ...I realized that the *intruder/s was/were* in the toilet. ...It filled me with horror and fear of *an intruder or intruders* being inside the toilet ... I believed that when the *intruder/s* came out of the toilet we would be in grave danger" [italics added]. The striking singular/plurals in Oscar's account suggest the possibility that his internalized primal scene combined parental couple may have invaded, contaminated, and highjacked his phantasy of romantic bliss.

Is there any other information that would support these hypotheses concerning Oscar's oedipal passions? From author John Carlin we learn that the Blade Runner's personality was suffused with what psychoanalysts might view as derivatives of oedipal conflicts:

> He bet all on romantic love and disappointment was his reward. One woman left ...and another took her place, but the pattern repeated itself time after time. From petulant possessiveness to frantic dependency, to hysterical fear of loss. No one could quite measure up. He had moments of light when he saw that he was driving himself— and them—mad, but he could not help himself. Jealously ate him up and he saw rivals everywhere. ...He was a man of extremes who had no legs, which gave a uniquely corrosive character to his insecurities about love and sex. (p. 128)

Besides suggesting the powerful presence of oedipal anxieties, Carlin's description of Oscar's love life raises the likelihood that the Blade Runner's oedipal development and later, related, adult passions, were problematically infused with more primitive *preoedipal* separation anxieties. The oral roots of these terrors are suggested in Carlin's phrase, "jealousy ate him up." What Carlin describes as petulant possessiveness, frantic dependency, and hysterical fear of loss resembles what toddlers feel when their mothers' rise to go to the bathroom (and what Edgar felt at the end of each of our sessions). In post-toddler preschool years, that fear of loss may become increasingly focused on unwelcome oedipal rivals.

Oscar's development had been arrested, Carlin writes. He "remained stuck in the weak, whimpering phase of puppy love. He had twin personalities" (p. 137). From a psychoanalytic perspective, one might say he was fixated to a significant degree in childhood oedipal love (and, to some extent, preoedipal love, hate, and fear). These more troubled, tumultuous aspects of his personality differed dramatically from the more rational, evolved, mature, impressive dimensions of his character structure.

Two-and-a-half weeks before Oscar shot Reeva, this oedipally-rooted jealousy erupted. Reeva communicated how upset she was when Oscar ruined her experience of her good friend's engagement party: "I was not flirting with anyone today. I feel sick that u suggested that and that u made a scene. ...I am scared of you sometimes ... and how you snap at me."

With a previous girlfriend, Samantha Taylor, Carlin reports, Oscar would also suddenly snap, becoming enraged with her or her friends, shouting abuse. He was furious when Sam went on a trip with a man, even though Oscar and she had broken up after she had accused him of having an affair with a Russian model in New York City. Jealous romantic triangles are a hallmark of oedipal complexities.

Photo by EPA / Frennie Shivambu CC by 2.0
November 4, 2012. Oscar and Reeva at the South African sports awards ceremony in Johannesburg.

In romantic relationships, Carlin wrote, Oscar kept swinging from wedding bell bliss to operatic despair. He panicked that his woman would abandon him, making him endure the grief of his mother's death all over again. Carlin focused on women's failure to live up to the Oscar's saintly ideal of his mother. That formulation is reminiscent of the Madonna-whore complex Freud described. In that oedipal configuration, women are seen as either sacred maternal figures or despised, debased sexual beings. Madonna mother in her sacred blue attire lovingly holds her precious baby while the prostitute version of this woman is in another room, shamelessly copulating with the child's libidinal rivals.

Carlin is surely at least partly correct in focusing on the tragedy of Oscar's beloved mother's death that occurred in his teens. Psychoanalytic psychologists might additionally emphasize oedipal and preoedipal roots of his ongoing reactions to that loss. Carlin's references to how self-centered, possessive, and suffocatingly demanding Oscar was with girlfriends accords with these earlier origins of his relational vulnerabilities.

Mrs. Steenkamp claimed Reeva had not had sex with Oscar during the three months they had known each other. If she is correct about the couple's restraint, one can imagine Oscar may have experienced frustration that could have influenced his unconscious fantasies. Given that guns can be aggressive phallic symbols in unconsciously generated imagery, Oscar could have been expressing thwarted sexual desire that awful night. In phallic fury, he may have unconsciously sought to explosively penetrate the final barrier separating him and Reeva, blasting his way through the despicable door that shut him out. In a dream, no harm would come from such a fantasy, even if it might have disturbed Oscar profoundly, the way my teenage patient Paul's dream of slitting his beloved sister's throat so horrified him. Even if Oscar's frustrated sexual impulses had spilled over into somnambulistic sex, things would not have been so dreadful.

It may be important to remind readers that this chapter contains considerable imaginative speculation, as in the previous paragraph. This chapter contemplates how things can be represented unconsciously. We cannot know whether these processes were actually operative in Oscar's case. They do occur in human minds, but this does not mean they did occur in the Blade Runner's psyche. These speculations are included in this book solely for the benefit of readers curious to know more about the range of ways in which unconscious representation can operate.

Judge Masipa wondered why Oscar fired his pistol through the bathroom door four times, rather than just once. The Court would obviously have much preferred for him to have merely provided a warning shot. In a paranoid-schizoid state of mind, rational cognition is absent. One simply seeks to eliminate threats. Additionally, dreams often contain multiple layers of symbolism that can both express and disguise deep desires and dreads. At one level, one might speculate, Oscar's four shots might have represented orgasmic rape and ejaculatory expulsion. One shot would not suffice to discharge pent-up passion. He had to shoot his whole load. The inhibitory door between him and Reeva needed to be smashed to smithereens. As on some wedding nights, there would be blood.

Sexsomnia

The more imaginative context of this chapter permits us to supplement ideas presented in Chapter 12, *Key to the Locked Door*. There, to explain why Reeva might have gone to the bathroom with her cellphone, slamming and locking the door behind her, I suggested Oscar might have dreamt of intruders. Sliding into a rapid eye movement sleep behavior disorder, he may have begun to enact his dream, attacking Reeva, mistakenly believing she was the dangerous invader, as so often happens in RBD. Now we can consider the additional possibility that in his sleep he might have begun to sexually molest Reeva, perhaps related to sexual frustration, causing her to flee to the toilet.

Atypical sexual behaviors of sleep can range from minor, even mutually enjoyable, transgressions to dangerous assaults. At the benign end of the continuum, Professor Schenck (2005, p. 374) described one man's girlfriend finding his sexual manner while asleep more aggressive and dominant than his waking behavior. Only when he was asleep did forceful, playful, biting and talking dirty occur. Although this woman recognized his *sleepsex* was "a little kinky and probably not normal," she encouraged him to incorporate these activities into his waking repertoire. She might have intuited that if he were more comfortable with such leanings, he would not have to suppress or repress them, and would not have to enact them during altered states of consciousness.

In one chapter of *Case Studies in Clinical Neurology* entitled "Sexsomnia and Obstructive Sleep Apnea," Professors Schenck & Mahowald shared the story of a thirty-two-year-old man who complained of "fondling my wife during sleep." His partner urged him to seek help for this problem that had begun four years earlier. At that time, he had started to snore and "would keep trying to hump me while he was asleep." She was "shocked" by this odd scenario that occurred up to four nights per week. Non-sexual *sleeptalking* also began appearing ever since he started snoring. He never remembered any of these events in the morning. She found this sleepsex offensive. It also disrupted her rest. She wondered whether she could remain married to him if these behaviors persisted.

Professor Schenck (2005, p. 370) described another man whom police would frequently find masturbating in front of a home. He would stare straight ahead at a window, glassy-eyed, looking confused, mumbling about a nude woman. He was convinced the shades were open, with the lights on, though the opposite was true. He was awake (somewhat) and also dreaming.

Dr. Schenck reviewed thirty-one cases of parasomnias involving sexuality. 80% were men, usually in their early thirties (approximately Oscar's age at the time of the tragedy). They had typically been exhibiting sexsomnia for almost ten years, *always with amnesia*. Snoring during sleepsex occurred in three patients with sleep apnea. In nearly half the cases, agitation or assault occurred. Nine cases involved sex with a minor. There were legal consequences in eleven cases. Injuries such as bruised penises or breasts, vaginal abrasions, lacerations, and scratch marks were common.

Inappropriate, vigorous, and harmful sleepsex with oneself or one's bed partner can also erupt during periods of *confusional arousal*, sometimes known as *sleep drunkenness*. Due to the almost universal amnesia accompanying confusional arousals, it is typically the bed partner who draws attention to these activities.

Confusional arousals are fairly common in children (17%) and adults under thirty-five years of age (4%). With children, episodes may seem bizarre and frighten parents. These youngsters often appear to be staring right through their parents. They may become more agitated when parents attempt to console them.

Sleepsex may go on for a long time. If the initiator wakes up, naturally or by force, s/he may simply roll over and go back to sleep, even if the partner wants to continue their engagement. Sometimes the initiator wakes up orgasming.

Might Oscar have tried to engage in sleepsex under the conditions of his allegedly abstinent relationship with Reeva? He would, of course, be amnesiac for any such sexsomnia. This possibility could fit with Reeva slamming the bathroom door and locking it. We do not, of course, have to be so specific in specifying the nature of the threat from which she may have sought refuge. Oscar could have mistaken her for a dangerous intruder, in common RBD manner. Alternatively, he could merely have been hollering at imagined intruders while brandishing his loaded Parabellum in a terrifying manner. Any of these possibilities could explain why Reeva carried her cellphone to the bathroom (giving her the option of calling for help if she could not get her lover to come to his senses).

As mentioned at the start of this chapter, many of its ideas would be complex and/or speculative. It nonetheless seemed worthwhile to venture into this imaginative investigative domain for the benefit of those readers who like more depth, challenge, mystery, ambiguity, nuance, and provocative ideas. One needs to cast the widest possible net to capture the broadest array of factors that could possibly have influenced Oscar to behave as he did that awful night. Most of the conceptual matrix we constructed in previous chapters derived from a relatively low inferential level. Here, in contrast, we allowed ourselves to entertain higher-level inferences. Both forms of discourse have their place. More theoretically informed conjectures appeal differentially to diverse audiences. Legal minds might want to focus on the ideas presented in earlier chapters, and those that will be discussed subsequently. Hopefully all readers may, nonetheless, find in this chapter some ideas that will peak their interest in learning more about complex mental states.

Chapter 16

SOCIALIZING BABIES, BOYS, AND MEN

*The sleepwalking 'werewolf' is in us all,
and we're all prone to have an isolated
episode of sleepwalking if a switching
error occurs. All we need is something to
destabilize our sleep.*
—Dr. Michel A. Cramer Bornemann
(cited by Bennett)

For his enlightening studies of masculinity, Ronald Levant received the American Psychological Association's Award for Distinguished Professional Contributions to Applied Research. In his acceptance speech, Dr. Levant situated his work in the context of Men's Studies scholars who challenged the prevailing view of masculinity as simply a universal expression of biology. These investigators interrogated traditional norms of maleness (e.g., dominance, aggression, extreme self-reliance, restrictive emotionality).

The conventional perspective that males are, by nature, less emotional than females is not evidence-based, Levant found. Boys are actually more emotionally reactive and expressive than girls until one year of age. By two, they are less verbally expressive than girls and, by six, less facially expressive. What happened over those few early years to render them less in touch with their feelings and less comfortable with sharing them?

Traditional male role socialization is "inherently traumatic," Levant states. It can cause mild to moderate alexithymia (inability to verbalize feelings). Discouraged from expressing affect, boys often do not develop awareness of many emotions, he theorized. Their greatest deficits typically pertain to identifying and expressing vulnerability (e.g., sadness, fear) or attachment (e.g., fondness, caring). This restricted emotionality may be adaptive in some highly competitive, aggressive environments, but causes problems in other areas (e.g., personal lives).

Traditional male socialization discourages men from seeking help with difficulties. A police officer contacted me for assistance with problems that were making his work life impossible. Someone connected with his employment had instructed him to call me. He said he would be mortified if any colleague ever knew he consulted a psychologist. His peers would rather "eat their guns" than get professional assistance, he stated.

Statistics bear out this policeman's grim view of his vocational world. In 2008 one hundred and forty-one policemen committed suicide in the USA. This is more than double the number killed by criminals. In Canada around the same time, more Ontario Provincial Police officers were dying by their own hands than in active duty. Likewise in the military, more American soldiers kill themselves than die from war injuries. From January to early May 2012, there was nearly one self-murder per day among active-duty troops. U.S. veterans suicide even more frequently—every eighty minutes. Unaddressed psychological problems can be deadly. Male acculturation can be a killer.

Detroit's police chief resigned a few years ago after an officer he had an affair with posted a picture on social media in which she was holding a handgun to her mouth.

Having learned the Chief was seeing another woman, this officer contemplated making the ultimate sacrifice. She was tempted to eat her gun rather than seek help with what might be seen as a contemporary insult that resonated with earlier, oedipally-based injury, jealousy, rage, and despair. Thankfully she merely dramatized her plight, thereby communicating it to others in a possible plea for help.

A few years ago, three National Hockey League 'enforcers' killed themselves in one year. Throughout their careers, they were rewarded for their hypermasculine, violent propensities and fighting abilities. Their suicides suggest they felt acknowledging their emotional needs to themselves, let alone to anyone else, would constitute unacceptable weakness that would throw their masculinity and maturity into grave doubt. Unlike the policewoman in Detroit, these men could neither bear nor share their distress. Seeking treatment was out of the question.

Athletes in hypermasculine sports like hockey and football are susceptible to concussions. These injuries may be inflicted by enforcers following orders from coaches, or they may be acquired in the game's 'ordinary' rough and tumble. These blows can cause brain damage, compromising cognition and decision-making. Military veterans with traumatic brain injury are at increased risk for suicide, though the severity of their brain damage does not necessarily correlate with increased suicide risk. Outside the realm of these highly aggressive, competitive endeavors, traditional male socialization causes at least metaphoric brain damage (restricted mental and emotional freedom) and facilitates similarly self-destructive endings.

Male socialization, cultural stereotypes, and ideologies create a masculine social script that is actually performable by both males and females who subscribe to these ideals and injunctions. A woman suggested to her friend that she should see me for psychotherapy. Her girlfriend declined, saying she could "do it herself," meaning she could resolve her problems independently. What she ended up doing by herself was firing a gun into her head. Her defensive style went way beyond the Detroit police officer's pantomime. It also went against the traditional truism that while women more often attempt suicide, men terminate their lives four times more frequently. In the male code of conduct, 'honor' requires falling upon one's sword rather than seeking help.

Given the cultural constraints of traditional masculinity, what chance was there that Oscar could have sought psychological assistance that may have reduced the probability of problems culminating in the events of February 14, 2013? As a highly dedicated, competitive, male athlete with a fondness for firearms, fine automobiles, and beautiful women, the likelihood of him seeking and obtaining psychotherapeutic help was not great.

Samantha Taylor, Oscar's girlfriend before Reeva, described her volatile relationship with him to authors Mandy Wiener & Barry Bateman. When Samantha did not want to speak with Oscar, he would telephone her sister ten to twenty times per day. He also called her brothers and mother, sometimes in the middle of the night. Like any traumatized youngster, he could not endure Winnicott's $x + y$ units of temporal separation. "We had broken up but he wouldn't acknowledge that." He was concerned that she was seeing another athlete, soccer player Quinton van der Burgh. Typically, Samantha's mother, Trish, bore the brunt of Oscar's outpourings. In her words:

> He was so emotionally unstable. ...I also knew that he had an angry streak. ...He cried continuously. ...I thought he was going to commit suicide. ...It carried on for months. ...I kept saying, 'Oz, you have to see a psychologist, you have to.' He used to promise all the time,

'No, I know I need help, I promise you, Trish, I promise you I will go to a psychologist.' He never did. In every conversation, he'd promise me he'd see a psychologist. He did book one in London, but he never went to the appointment.

If socialization and cultural pressures had not worked against Oz seeking psychotherapeutic assistance for his extreme jealousy with women, his emotional volatility, impulsiveness, difficult aspects of his childhood, and so forth, might treatment have reduced the likelihood that he would end up firing bullets into that bathroom door on that dreadful night in 2013? If in addition to his fear of intruders, Oscar's insecurity, anger, stress, and fear of abandonment in all important relationships due to foundational anxieties from his earlier years were factors disturbing his sleep that night, it is possible that psychotherapy could have helped him to resolve those issues sufficiently such that he would have slept better, rather than sliding down a slippery slope from dream to nightmare to violent dream enactment.

Similar reasoning would apply to other cases, such as that of Kenneth Parks. Like Oscar, Ken was inclined to seek physical relief rather than confronting his anxiety and other problems in psychotherapy or elsewhere. In lieu of keeping his promise to his wife that he would confess to his grandmothers about the mess he had gotten himself and his family into, he elected to play rugby. If Kenneth could have worked on his fears of being judged, humiliated, and abandoned, he might have been able to deal better and sooner with his grandmothers, his insomnia, and his imminent confession to his in-laws. If he had sought help as soon as he got into gambling difficulties or, preferably, long before he turned to the horses in hopes that they would solve his problems, his mother-in-law might be alive today, and Kenneth's marriage might not have ended.

Even in Kenneth's relatively affluent country, Canada, the government does not encourage citizens to seek psychotherapeutic assistance. Provincial health care plans do not cover visits to clinical psychologists practicing independently, as most of them must do. By this neglect, the government transmits a powerful message that psychological health is nowhere near as important as physical health that is more fully covered.

Ironically, after passing judgment, the courts required both Oscar and Ken to engage in psychotherapy. How much better it would have been if male socialization and government policy endeavored, prior to tragedies, to encourage citizens to attend to mental health issues in the spirit of early intervention and prevention rather than favoring neglect, denial, and belated interventions. A stitch in time saves nine.

The day will come when seeking psychological assistance will be much more widely seen by individuals, cultures, subcultures, and governments as a strength, not a weakness. Psychotherapy will be viewed as something that saves money and, more importantly, lives. When that blessed time arrives, there will be far fewer crimes of passion, and far less police officers, soldiers, veterans, and athletes committing suicide. In the meantime, many of our governments continue to be complicit in these tragedies.

Chapter 17

Why Did Oscar's Defense Not Raise the Dreaming and Parasomnia Possibility?

With the role of ever increasing causes, manifestations, and consequences of sleep-related violence comes an opportunity for sleep medicine specialists to educate the general public and practicing clinicians as to the occurrence and nature of such behaviors, and their successful treatment.

– Mahowald et al., Handbook of Clinical Neurology

The Long Winding Road That Leads to Understanding

Perhaps the first documented case of sleep killing concerned medieval Silesian woodcutter, Bernard Schedmaizig who woke abruptly after a few hours. In a state of confusional arousal, believing he saw an intruder by his bed, he picked up his axe, inadvertently killing his wife who had been slumbering peacefully beside him.

In the 1878 *Journal of Mental Science*, Scottish physician David Yellowless described how a young man with a history of sleep terrors smashed his eighteen-month-old son against a wall during the night. He had mistaken his toddler for a wild beast about to attack. Intending to protect his nuclear family, he instead killed its most vulnerable member. In a similar, recent instance of gross confusion between inner and outer realities, Professor Rosalind Cartwright described the case of a parasomniac woman who threw her baby out a window, believing her house was on fire. Another man dragged his wife out of bed, certain that their mattress was on fire.

I am inclined to speculate that in some parasomnias, in addition to neurophysiological vulnerabilities allowing for temporary disruption of the gating mechanism that would ordinarily shut off access to motility while dreaming, there could also be underlying psychodynamic issues predisposing to violent phantasies and related actions. Many men feel a disturbing sense of loss, disruption, unease, and anger when additions to their families take away significant amounts of their wives' attention to them. In the case cited by Dr. Yellowless, the man who killed his eighteen-month-old infant may have been struggling with unacceptable, rivalrous, aggressive feelings toward his offspring whose emergence onto the family scene may have felt like an attack on the superior status quo ante. In his dream, these murderous reactions may have been represented by and projected into the animated image of the dangerous wild beast. That animal could symbolize what Carl Jung referred to as the Shadow to the man's otherwise civilized Persona. He may have tried to repress these violent impulses but, in what Freud famously described as *the return of the repressed*, these action tendencies reincarnated in the powerfully animated image of the beast rising from beneath the floor (i.e., from the unconscious). As he struggled to protect his family, this man became a wild beast.

This affective discomfort and resultant aggression is tragically common in men due to their acculturation that so often seems to begin dimming their emotional awareness and expressiveness as early as in the first year of life. This man's animal impulses may have been too strong to be successfully sequestered for long in his unconscious. In the form of the beast, they may have exploded through the repression barrier. If he had not been predisposed to parasomnia, and/or if he had been able to tolerate his emotions better (or had access to psychotherapy), his dream might have been merely an unsettling, ultimately productive phenomenon. Analyzing the fantasy it embodied, he might have been able to come to comprehend his troubling feelings and gradually grow emotionally from that understanding.

Postpartum depression may lead some deluded women to kill their offspring, perhaps mistakenly believing this murder is for their children's own good. Men may be more inclined to struggle with postpartum anger, sometimes related to jealousy of the baby's intimate relationship with mother. Recall how Kenneth Parks' original adoration of his daughter disappeared after just a few weeks. He became unwilling to participate in her care. Eventually he refused to even hold her. Not long thereafter he was exporting murderous impulses to his in-laws' home.

Some research evidence supports the idea that repression of unacceptable aggressive impulses may be associated with rapid eye movement sleep behavior disorder. In 2005, Maria Livia Fantini and her co-workers found that compared with control subjects, RBD patients had elevated aggressive dream content despite normal daytime aggressiveness. Prominent sleep specialists, such as Drs. Schenck, Lee, Cramer Bornemann, and Mahowald (2009), frequently note that spouses of violent RBD patients often say partners' nocturnal aggression is completely discordant from their pleasant daytime personalities. The research conducted by Fantini and her colleagues would lead one to wonder whether those RBD patients might also repress aggression more than most people do. Those disowned impulses would then manifest in dreams and, perhaps, parasomnia.

In the December 2010 issue of *Brain*, Francesca Siclari and her co-workers presented a large number of cases of sleep violence that have been reported in the professional literature. One man they described was sleeping around a campfire. Suddenly he felt he was being burnt. Jumping to his feet, he grabbed an axe, then killed a man close to him. Apart from this man's psychobiological vulnerability to parasomnia, one might speculate that he might also have suffered from homophobia—another common accompaniment to male discomfort with feelings. Despite it being lovely to camp with others, it can also be a disequilibrating experience for some of us due to our unconscious, 'burning' dreads and desires pertaining to closeness with men. Fearing intimacy, boundary crossing, and sexual intrusion, we may have to defensively flip the situation so that instead of feeling threatened, we become the threatening, violent intruders. If these anxieties and defenses can be contained within a dream, all is well. If that dream can be understood (for example, in therapy), so much the better. If, however, dream enactment occurs, major problems may ensue.

Another person described by Siclari and her team was gripped during his sleep by a vivid image of soldiers attacking his daughter. He left the house, seized an axe, entered her bedroom, and tried to 'defend' his child, striking her with his weapon. In a similar story with a much better outcome, recall my little patient, Edgar, who created a play scene in which soldiers fired at a baby girl who perhaps represented Edgar's sister, Sue-Yin. Edgar was able to introduce the protective figure of a mother who defended this child from the violent military. Edgar had the benefit of a parent who brought him to psychotherapy. He therefore had a venue for expressing his feelings rather than having to act them out in potentially harmful ways. The man who killed his daughter, mistakenly believing he was protecting her from soldiers, did not have the benefit of such a therapeutic space for processing his feelings.

Another person that Siclari et al. described dreamt that burglars were murdering his family. He therefore grabbed two guns and fired ten shots, inadvertently killing his father and brother. His mother got away with non-lethal injuries. Yet another man dreamt that two Japanese soldiers were chasing him and his wife through the jungle. He strangled one soldier and kicked another. In actuality, he was strangling his wife to death.

All these accused individuals discussed by Siclari et al. were acquitted. In other cases where a parasomnia defense has been used, it has not always been successful. In these latter instances, the accused killers were convicted, rightly or wrongly.

In a March 23, 2010 New York Times article entitled *Violence in the Land of Sleep,* Roger Ekirch reflected on the fact that sleep violence has long been a source of consternation. As early as the 14th century, the Council of Vienne in southern France reported sleep murders. That discussion was echoed in the following, Fifteenth Century in a Spanish treatise that spoke of "murderous sleepwalkers," specifically referring to one well-known English case. In 1678 another English incident gained international attention when Colonel Cheyney Culpepper, a known habitual sleepwalker, fired his blunderbuss at a guard. Culpepper claimed he committed this crime in a somnambulistic state. He produced fifty witnesses to attest to the wide range of activities he had performed while sleeping. Deemed insane, he was convicted, then pardoned by King James II.

By the 1800's, as newspaper circulation increased, cases of sleep violence became more familiar to the public. Medical evidence now played an integral role in trials. In their efforts to exonerate clients, lawyers called upon psychiatric testimony. One Kentucky defendant, convicted in 1879 of shooting a hotel porter, was later freed on the grounds that he had not been permitted to "prove by medical experts that persons asleep sometimes act as if awake."

Unlike in that Kentucky acquittal, no one forbid Oscar's defence team from raising the possibility that he suffered from parasomnia on Saint Valentine's Day, 2013. Given that there is such a long history of accused persons being defended on such grounds, why did no one raise this possibility? Let us consider several possible reasons.

Insufficient Knowledge of Parasomnia in the Legal and Mental Health Professions

In an article published in *Psychology Today* on January 2, 2013 entitled *Dangerous Dreamers: Can Sleep Disorders Explain Brutal Murder or Unexpected Suicide?*, David K. Randall, author of *Dreamland: Adventures in the Strange Science of Sleep,* referred to a 2002 paper in the *Minnesota Law Review* by Deborah Denno. She argued that the way courts view sleep needs reform. The foundations of the criminal code pertaining to unconscious and involuntary states such as sleepwalking have not been thoroughly updated since the 1950s when scientific understanding of sleep was rudimentary. Professor Denno proposed a number of improvements, including the idea of degrees of consciousness and a new category of semi-voluntary acts. Courts have done little to reach uniform standards since that article was published, Randall stated.

Given the legal system's inadequate scientific knowledge concerning sleep, dreaming, consciousness, and intentionality, Oscar's defense counsel, expert witnesses, and judge may not have been sufficiently familiar with the possibility that he could have been acting under conditions of a complex sleep and dreaming disorder on that awful night. Parasomnias are far less widely known and understood than one might hope. Books such as this one will gradually improve this situation.

Rather than raising the possibility of parasomnia, the mental health specialists who informed the court at Oscar's trial discussed his current post-traumatic stress disorder, anxiety, and depression. In terms of pre-existing personality organization, one expert suggested there were two Oscars. One was the remarkable man the world knew and admired prior to the killing. The other subself was the romantically insecure, possessive, impulsive, aggressive individual known only to himself, intimate female partners, and a few others in his social circle. The Blade Runner may have had a pre-existing anxiety disorder involving heightened vigilance and startle response but, the experts believed, that condition was not sufficiently strong to be a significant factor in the tragedy. Any such propensities would not have prevented him from knowing the difference between right and wrong.

Focussed on matters other than parasomnia, these experts may not have realized that there were many gaping holes in Oscar's otherwise coherent narrative that might have reflected his having transitioned from an innocent dream of convenience, to a nightmare, and then to a more serious parasomniac state. In those latter, paranoid-schizoid frames of mind, it is survival, not more nuanced moral matters that matter. The kill or be killed mindset occludes all other, more evolved, empathic considerations.

The mature, awake Oscar knew right from wrong. He spent much time helping those less fortunate than himself. In a nightmare, one is in a completely different state of consciousness. In that condition, one's intrapsychic situation and mental capacities diverge considerably from everyday life. In that paranoid realm, one focuses exclusively on protecting oneself and loved ones. One's aim is to simply eliminate perceived threats as quickly as possible.

Researchers at Stanford, the University of Minnesota, and other centers of excellence have been trying to address the lack of knowledge concerning parasomnia in medicine, psychiatry, neurology, psychology, and the law. The public, too, is typically unaware of the frequency and nature of sleep violence. This book will hopefully contribute to raising awareness of these matters.

Dr. Mark Mahowald, a neurologist at the University of Minnesota, in conjunction with researchers from Stanford University, conducted a study published in *Sleep Medicine,* reporting that nearly two percent of adults admit to acting violently during their sleep. That statistic translates into a very large number of citizens. Since embarrassment may prevent more people from admitting to such behavior, the actual incidence of sleep violence may be higher, he believed.

In another study, Harvey Moldofsky and his co-workers reported harmful behavior by 59% of patients at a sleep clinic with nocturnal terrors and sleepwalking. Guilleminault and his team found harmful behavior in 70% of patients with nocturnal wanderings of different aetiologies. These clinic-based percentages may overestimate the prevalence of violence in patients with parasomnia since individuals manifesting such behavior are more likely to consult sleep clinics.

Attention Blindness

From the time the police arrived at the scene of the tragedy at Oscar's home right through to the end of his trial, and even to this day, the question on everyone's mind was always the same: Was the Blade Runner simply trying to protect himself and Reeva from burglars, or did he knowingly murder her? Hilton Botha, the investigating detective, was certain this incident was just another crime of passion. Prosecuting attorney Gerrie Nel agreed. The women's section of South Africa's ruling party (The African National Congress) and other women's groups were also convinced Mr. Botha and the prosecution were correct. They wanted Judge Masipa to punish the Blade Runner severely in order to send a clear message to society that crimes of gender violence will not be tolerated. Others argued that in a crime-ridden culture, Oscar's story made perfect sense. The fact that he suffered from a physical handicap and, at the time, was not wearing his prosthetic legs, increased his vulnerability, leading to his being more frightened and more likely to defend himself with his gun.

Around the world, people followed this shocking, compelling case with intense interest. They debated and wondered which of these two narratives would be supported by the evidence and the judiciary. With the entire realm of possible explanations taken up by these two hotly contested possibilities, there was little or no room for alternative reasoning.

When our attention is focused on one thing, or on one of two possibilities, one of which may be strongly favored, it can be difficult or impossible for any other option to enter the picture. Recent studies of *inattentional blindness* provide striking evidence of this phenomenon. Harvard psychologists Daniel Simons and Christopher Chabris instructed subjects watching a basketball film to count how many times the ball passed between members of one team. Half the observers did not notice anything unusual. In reality, a gorilla (a person wearing a costume) had sauntered into the middle of the court. This ape stopped and thumped his chest for nine long seconds. After this dramatic display, the gorilla sauntered away.

In Carpenter's 2001 article in the American Psychological Association's *Monitor on Psychology*, Professor Christopher Chabris commented on these studies: "I think every serious person in psychology has always believed that we don't consciously perceive everything that happens to us. The shocking thing was that you could show that so little is being perceived." Dr. Brian Scholl, a cognitive psychologist at Yale, added: "This research is showing us something we didn't think was the case—that we can fail to perceive very major things going on right in front of our eyes. These studies are truly surprising for both scientists and lay people because they're so at odds with how we assumed vision worked."

Cognition functions similarly to perception. While most people are shocked upon first hearing about inattentional blindness, they might be less surprised by the idea that when one is focused on one explanatory theory (or two), one's mind might be blind to other possibilities. This, I believe, was the case in the public's mind with respect to the charges against Oscar. The media, and virtually everyone else, were entranced by the unfolding, high stakes drama in 'the trial of this century'. Each observer focused primarily on one of what were generally viewed as the only two possible explanations: murder or self-defense. There was little or no space for the third option, namely that Oscar was enacting a nightmare. Studies on inattention blindness can help us to realize that we may have watched the Blade Runner's case unfold with mindsets that made it impossible for us to conceive of any explanation beyond the two that were on the table. This constricted cognition may even have affected many who knew about parasomnia. Caught up in the fiery debate between the other two contending explanations, the possibility of parasomnia did not come up in court.

Automatism

The only moment where anyone in the courtroom gave any attention to possible involuntarism was when they grappled with whether Oscar had intentionally fired four shots or had done so reflexively after having been startled by a sound emanating from the toilet chamber. In the Blade Runner's words: "The accident was that I discharged my firearm in the belief that an intruder was coming out to attack me. ...My understanding is that I did not intend to discharge my firearm. ...I fired my firearm before I could think."

Attempting to catch Oscar in a contradiction, prosecutor Nel, in his closing argument, demanded to know what his defense was. "Is it putative self-defence" [BW: mistakenly thinking he had to protect himself and Reeva from intruders]? Or "Is it an act of sane automatism" [BW: firing reflexively when startled by a noise]? To me, it does not seem that those two possibilities are mutually exclusive. It could be a consistent, plausible narrative for Oscar to argue that he approached what he thought were intruders, armed to shoot if necessary, if they did not heed his screams for them to get out of his home. Then, when startled by a sound that he interpreted to mean the home invaders were about to emerge from the toilet chamber to harm him and his lover, he reflexively opened fire.

This reconciliation of opposites is consistent with the testimony of Professor Wayne Derman, the physician for the South African Paralympic Team on which Oscar participated. Dr. Derman was very familiar with the Blade Runner's anxiety. He had medicated him in the past for sleep disorder. Professor Derman described him as having an exaggerated startle response that typically triggers flight-fight reactions. When Prosecutor Nel challenged Dr. Derman about Oscar's claim that he "was not thinking" when he pulled the trigger, the physician responded that the unconscious part of the brain comes into play in such situations, especially in individuals with higher anxiety, and that accounts for their inability to think.

Defence counsel submitted that Oscar could not be held liable for a reflex discharge caused by his increased startle response. Judge Masipa disagreed: "The latter concept has the hallmark of a defence of non-pathological insanity, as it gives the impression that the accused had no control over his action when he fired the shots at the door. That this cannot be, is clear from the steps that the accused took from the moment he heard the sounds of the window opening to the time he fired the four shots. There was no lapse of memory or any confusion on the part of the accused. On his own version he froze, then decided to arm himself and go to the bathroom. In other words he took a conscious decision."

In contrast to Judge Masipa's everyday reasoning, we know from many trials, such as that of Kenneth Parks, that arming oneself and even traveling a considerable distance, then entering a home and killing someone, does not necessarily involve making what we normally regard as conscious decisions. If Oscar, like Ken, had been in a parasomniac state, then he would not have been making what we generally consider to be fully conscious decisions. In her deliberations, Judge Masipa continued: "He knew where he kept his firearm and he knew where his bathroom was. He noticed that the bathroom window was open, which is something that confirmed his correctness about having heard the window open earlier. This is inconsistent with lack of criminal capacity." Again we have clearly seen from cases such as Kenneth Parks' that one can know where lethal weapons are and navigate precisely to even a distant location without necessarily being conscious in the ordinary meaning of that word. As a result, one can be found *not criminally responsible* for the ensuing tragedy.

Before delivering her verdict, Judge Masipa articulated something of profound importance: "What must be borne in mind however, is that the conclusion which is reached, whether it be to convict or to acquit must account for all the evidence." In contrast to the rigorous requirements of this crucial principle, she acknowledged earlier that: "There are indeed a number of aspects in the case which do not make sense." She proceeded to list the four striking points defying comprehension that I have discussed in detail. Lacking sufficient knowledge of the psychology and neurophysiology of sleep and dreaming, and their disorders, the Court was unable to account for all the evidence. They therefore could not reach an ideal or, one might argue, a correct and adequate verdict.

In dreams and in the unconscious more generally, Freud emphasized, contradictions easily coexist, with little or no attempt to reconcile them. Oscar's testimony contained contradictions. In one breath he told the Court that he did not shoot into the bathroom and that he pulled the trigger, firing four bullets through the door. To the extent that he was still at least partly in his dream state when he opened fire, 'he' did not really pull the trigger but, also, he did. That is, his dream enactment self launched the bullets, but his rational, mature, awake, fully cognizant self did not.

Unfortunately for Oscar, Judge Masipa, like prosecutor Nel, and most of us, thought exclusively in terms of secondary process cognition as she grappled with implausible aspects of the Blade Runner's argument. In her judgement she wrote: "The accused was clearly not being candid with the court when he said that he had no intention to shoot at anyone as he had a loaded firearm to his hand, ready to shoot." Not being candid is far less damning than Nel's characterizing Oscar as a liar. It does, however, seem to me that the Olympic athlete may have been candid. He only intended to shoot if the intruders did not respond to his shouting at them to leave. By his account, he did not fire until he was startled by sounds of movement in the toilet stall that caused him to believe that lethal harm to him and Reeva was imminent. At that instant, he pulled the trigger reflexively, feeling there was no time to entertain alternative courses of action.

Even with respect to that relatively minor issue as to whether Oscar pulled the trigger voluntarily, reflexively, or as a non-insane involuntarism, litigation attorney David Dadic told journalists Mandy Wiener and Barry Bateman that involuntary action is "a well-known defence in our law but one that's not easily accepted by our courts and usually difficult to prove." Associate Criminal Law Professor James Grant concurred: Oscar's "testimony seems to be raising this [automatism] defence. ...A claim of involuntariness is a difficult one because our courts assume that ordinary conduct is voluntary." Again, this possibility of involuntarism was only being considered, and then merely briefly, in relation to the moment when Oscar pulled the trigger. No one was raising this idea in relation to the entire course of tragic events that transpired that night. I am raising that likelihood. It needs to be seriously contemplated.

Not only in South Africa are courts unaware of, or unreceptive to, the defence of involuntariness. Professor Cartwright notes that few of those accused with sleepwalking crimes in the USA have been acquitted using a somnambulism defence when a sleep expert has testified for the prosecution. Furthermore, she noted, many accused of such crimes are represented by public defenders who generally have little knowledge and limited resources with which to mount a parasomnia defense based on the growing body of research evidence.

Another American sleep specialist, Dr. Michel A. Cramer Bornemann, told author David K. Randall that judges and lawyers routinely scoff at the notion that a sane person could commit a complex, violent act while asleep. Dr. Bornemann cited a San Diego fisherman who claimed he had stabbed his girlfriend to death while dreaming he was gutting a shark. He was found guilty of murder. Dismissing the defense, the judge proclaimed: "This whole business of committing a murder while sleepwalking. ...I think the best word is sophistry."

If the courts are generally unreceptive even to relatively minor concerns as to whether Oscar pulled the trigger intentionally or reflexively, then they would not be inclined to think that the enormous implausibilities and contradictions in his testimony might be due to his having been in a parasomniac mind set throughout the entire tragic incident. With greater understanding of the scientific knowledge derived from intensive study of sleep, dreaming, and their disorders, key issues that were incomprehensible to the judicial system become understandable. Rendered intelligible at last, crucial, major components of the trial testimony and evidence, rather than just being noted, overlooked, acknowledged as incomprehensible, or dismissed, can now be used to reach a more valid verdict.

Chapter 18

SURELY EVERYONE KNOWS WHETHER THEY ARE ASLEEP OR AWAKE

*The art of art, the glory of expression
and the sunshine of the light of letters,
is simplicity.*

—Walt Whitman

Oscar himself never suggested he acted unconsciously. That could be another reason why his defense team did not raise this possibility. He never proposed he was anything other than fully awake throughout the events in question. Such self-report with regard to his state of consciousness, whatever it might actually have been, is hardly surprising. Sleep terror and other forms of dream enactment imagery can be so vivid and convincing that sufferers believe they are completely conscious. When concerned people tell these parasomniacs to wake up, they may insist they are actually already wide awake. This phenomenon is astounding, important, and relevant to Oscar's case.

The idea that one can actually be dreaming, but think one is fully awake is so significant in many cases including, I believe, the Blade Runner's, that I want to cite compelling examples from Professor Schenck's (2007) oeuvre:

I'll wake up in a state of shock where there is either an intruder [*BW: recall Oscar's conviction that there was an intruder in his home.*] or there is something that I can't explain in the room. ... My heart rate will increase to the point where it feels like the most powerful adrenaline charge you could get from being the most afraid of something that you could be. [*BW: Surely Oscar's adrenalin was supercharged that night.*] I would let out a scream and usually that is when I wake myself up. [*BW: Freud's protective night watchman.*] When I come out of it, I am usually breathing heavy and my heart rate is way up and I'm a little bit disoriented. I then collect my thoughts. From there, usually I can rationalize the situation, understand where I am and what I am doing, and go back to sleep. ...I'll think it over because it really leaves an impact on my mind. (p. 243)

In marked contrast to those times when this man's screaming woke him and he gradually brought himself back to reality, on other occasions:

I have argued the point with my dad. I have said, 'No, no, *this was real. This wasn't a dream* this time. *This was real.*' We would sit and argue for 15 minutes on whether something was there or not. (p. 244, italics added).

One can imagine that Oscar would argue with equal intensity that he, too, had been fully awake in the middle of the night of September 14, 2013.

In keeping with the idea that auditory stimulation can frequently trigger night terrors in those predisposed to them, this man continued:

A lot of times, hearing something will coincide with what I see. The way I think of it is that I'll hear something strange that is not normal to the environment that I'm sleeping in, and my mind will instantly dream some type of thing for me to see. [*BW: Recall Oscar believing he heard the window sliding open, then hearing ominous movement in the toilet chamber. As with Dr. Schenck's patient, this auditory stimulation was, I believe, immediately dreamt into concrete imagery by Oscar.*] For instance, we lived in an apartment complex where we were on the third floor. I had episodes for maybe a month straight whenever there was ice cracking on the roof. I would get up two to three times a night with this noise and my dad would come running out and say, 'It's just the ice on the roof,' and I would say, 'No, there is somebody up there.' He would have to convince me that there was no one on the roof. At the time, I thought, 'I am nuts, I'm paranoid.' Then I convinced myself that it was ice. I'd go back to sleep and a couple of hours later, I'd be up again. (p. 244)

In keeping with the high frequency of fear of intruders penetrating these parasomniacs' homes (as in Oscar's case), Professor Schenck's patient reported:

Someone is usually attacking, someone is breaking into the house. ...There is usually a good reason for what I do. *In the dream itself, of what I remember, I am usually already up and doing something* [*BW: Just like Oscar thought he was up bringing in fans, closing drapes, putting Reeva's jeans over the LED light, etc.*] and that is the point where I remember the dream.

...Either I'm real courageous and I'm doing something to save my family or myself [*BW: like Oscar endeavoring to protect himself and Reeva*], or I'm scared to death and I'm running from something. Either way, it involves fear and action. Desperate action. ...*I thought I was awake and this was real.* It wouldn't alarm me if I thought I was asleep and dreaming. I could have rationalized the whole thing and said that I was dreaming, but it was there and *I thought it was real.* (pp. 245-246, italics added)

We can be sure that Oscar, too, would argue that he was fully awake on that fateful night in 2013. Hopefully this book, including the discussion it may stimulate, will enable the Blade Runner to entertain and evaluate the alternative, dreaming and parasomnia hypothesis.

Another man told Dr. Schenck: "I've had a couple of roommates in the past and convinced them that somebody was actually there, and had gotten them up to take a look. *This was really real*" (p. 254, italics added).

The vivid, *hyper-real* dreams that one man experienced during his sleep terrors convinced him he must be awake. When his wife would try to wake him up, he would shout that he was *already awake*:

He jumps up, he'll jump right straight up on his feet and then I grab him and I yell, 'Bob, Bob, wake up!' at the top of my lungs. He's always yelling at the top of his lungs, '*I am awake, I am awake!*' One night I almost pulled his arm out of its socket trying to hold him down" (pp. 273-274, italics added).

A female patient told of a distressing night during which she 'woke' up often, fearing an intruder was present. She repeatedly checked various rooms and the locks on doors to make sure they were intact and protecting her.

> I awoke at some point and thought there were several men outside (I *saw* them outside my window). I was sure they were trying to figure a way to break in. I dressed and started closing and locking windows. I did return to sleep and awoke again, thinking the same threat was lurking. (p. 251)

Another man told Dr. Schenck that he usually *felt wide-awake* during his night terrors. They were experienced as being 'so vivid' and occurring '*in real time*.' After these terrors occurred, he typically tried to convince people in the room that he had been *fully awake* and what he had seen and responded to were actual events with *real, not imagined* people. It was completely clear to observers that he was asleep. He determined to find 'evidence' left by the intruder that would serve as undeniable proof of these trespassers' existence.

Another individual who had eventually come to be less convinced that he had been awake when certain events transpired told Dr. Schenck: "*I would wake up thinking I had been awake*, but I still must have been asleep and seeing people outside and people talking and things like that." (p. 336, italics added)

> When I recounted to my family and friends [what I eventually had to concede were] these very vivid dreams that I would have, and *people were very astounded by the detail*, and it almost became that I had parallel lives, where I'd be like, 'let me tell you what happened while you were sleeping. I had this occurrence.' (pp. 287-290, italics added)

Another parasomniac's sister told Dr. Schenck:

He had superhuman strength and so much energy and he would look at you and say, *'I'm not asleep.'* He'd say, 'See that over there?' and 'It's going to get you!' and *'Don't tell me I'm asleep because I'm awake.'* But he wasn't awake, because he could still see whatever he was scared of and pretty much ever since he was a little kid, he used to have very weird dreams and sometimes he'd get up and tell you and still be in it and tell you about it. It was very scary that he'd leave the house or you'd be sound asleep and he'd burst into the room or he'd be out in the hallway screaming. [*BW: Might Reeva also have been scared by Oscar's similar behavior? Hollering figured prominently in the Blade Runner's description of his behavior that night.*] And then when we were in our twenties, we both lived in the same city. We didn't live together, but I remember he had some pretty freaky dreams then too.

He'd always tell you that he wasn't asleep. He would tell you this fantastic thing that was happening right now, and he'd look at you right in the face and say, 'and you know *I'm not asleep.'* Cause' [sic] you'd say 'wake up, wake up.' (p. 297, italics added)

One can be quite sure that Oscar, likewise, would argue that he was not asleep when he confronted what he was certain were home invaders.

Another patient *thought he was awake* but was not as sure of that as the above described individuals. This man was prone to sleepeating.

A lot of times I'll be dreaming and I'll get out of bed and I really don't know if I'm dreaming for sure, or if I'm up. I go to the refrigerator right away. But I don't know for sure if it's a dream or if I'm awake or what." (Do you eat?) "I have been doing it all the time, right after I wake up from dreaming. I go to the refrigerator and get something to eat. I don't know if I'm still dreaming or if I'm awake. I think *I'm awake*, but not for sure." (p. 352, italics added)

Another individual could not be certain whether he was asleep or awake:

I awoke, well, I can't say for sure if I woke up. I saw two figures standing at the end of the bed and ...I was going like this, trying to kick them back. Then I started coming-to, sort of becoming aware of the surroundings of the room, and I saw a shadow of the door, the door was partly opened and there was a shadow there, and that shadow I thought was part of one of the figures I thought I had seen (in my dream). The other figure, I don't know what happened. I kicked. I just started kicking—the big faceless, shapeless figures were still there." (p. 113)

Blurred awareness as to whether one is asleep or awake can also be observed in the laboratory. Professor Schenck described one woman who on two occasions in his lab, after precipitous slow-wave sleep arousals, while appearing alert, awake, and oriented, reported still being in a dream. These events illustrated *waking mentation concurrent with an active dream state*, immediately after sudden arousals from deep non-REM sleep, when thinking should be sluggish and dream recall absent. "It seems that anything can and does happen during sleep and in the transition from sleep to awakening (but ...what exactly is an awakening?)," Dr. Schenck wrote (p. 249).

"It has become apparent that the all-or-none concept of state determination [BW: i.e., *being governed by*] (wakefulness, nonrapid eye movement sleep, rapid eye movement sleep) does not always exist, and that ambiguous, multiple, or rapid oscillation of state-determining variables appear in a wide variety of experimental and clinical situations" (p. 302). Elsewhere, Dr. Schenck noted: "This man may not always be waking up from sleep, but may actually at times be waking up from a dream-within-a-dream. Sometimes he may simultaneously wake up from sleep, his dream, and his dream-within-a-dream. Complicated shifts in an uncertain, fluctuating realm of sleep, dreams, and weird awakenings"(p. 112).

In short, people, and I believe Oscar Pistorius was one such individual, can feel absolutely certain they are wide-awake. They may insist on this 'fact' adamantly during and long after the episode. It may, however, be obvious to onlookers, though not to the individual involved, that the person in question was asleep, or awake and asleep simultaneously, enacting a dream. Clearly this finding is not only interesting but also highly significant, particularly in cases such as that of the Blade Runner.

Despite believing he was awake, Oscar continued to be baffled about what happened that dreadful night, even though he had a comprehensive, credible story, albeit one that included gigantic enigmas that no one to date has been able to resolve. Despite those enormous anomalies that the Bail Magistrate and later the Judge could only underscore, but not understand, the Blade Runner, and ultimately the Court, believed his original account (which, I believe, may well have been accurate but seriously incomplete). Nonetheless, long after having been convicted of homicide, Oscar shared in a British television interview: "I always think 'How did this possibly happen? How could this have happened?" His enduring bafflement is very important. Those same questions that continued to torment him have also seized my attention.

Only the dreaming and parasomnia hypotheses enable us to respond to Oscar's poignant queries.

Kenneth Parks did not raise the possibility that he killed his mother-in-law in his sleep. This peculiar idea never occurred to him. Despite its after-the-fact obviousness, this notion never entered his head until his defence team raised it. When they suggested this might have happened, only very gradually did Ken eventually come to see that their formulation seemed capable of making sense of what had transpired. Nonetheless, even after his preliminary trial, he continued to be convinced of his alternative explanation that someone had entered his home, drugged him, then dragged him to his car prior to driving him to his in-laws'. Inside their abode, Ken reasoned, he must have started to revive and realized his kidnapper was murdering his mother-in-law. While struggling to protect her, his hands were severely cut. Kenneth admitted there were problems with this narrative (as there were with Oscar's story). Although his tale was far-fetched, it did not seem much more so to him than the idea of him not being able to remember driving fourteen miles, then attacking his beloved in-laws, all in his sleep. We can imagine that Oscar will initially be as incredulous as Kenneth Parks was when he hears that he may have been in a parasomniac state when he killed his lover. He will be inclined to stick to his original story that is infinitely more reasonable than the wild narrative that Ken Parks constructed and thus so much harder to relinquish despite its inability to account for major anomalies that continued to fuel Oscar's agonizing question, "How did this possibly happen? How could this have happened?" Given that he was unable to come up with any explanation for the glaring gaps in his narrative right to the end of his long trial, the dreaming and parasomnia hypotheses have to be regarded as providing the only existing, viable, necessary understanding of these enormous enigmas.

Poolside Parasomnia?

The idea that killers would not believe they could have terminated someone's life while sleepwalking, that they would resist that idea, is also well illustrated by the Scott Falater case. Unlike Kenneth Parks who had not finished high school, had been fired, and was heavily in debt, Scott was an electrical engineer working in a middle management position in a large American corporation. He had no financial problems. Around 10:30 p.m. on January 16, 1997, his neighbor, Greg Koons, was not yet asleep. He heard some commotion at Scott's residence. Climbing the wall separating their properties, Greg was able to see a body lying near the swimming pool. He imagined there must have been a party and that this person passed out from too much alcohol. At that moment, a light turned on in an upstairs window in Scott's home. Greg could see Scott moving from room to room. Next, Scott appeared by the pool. He raised his hand to restrain one of his dogs from jumping up on him. Standing over the body, he had "a blank staring look." Then he pushed the supine figure into the water.

Greg called the police. Upon hearing the ruckus the officers were making downstairs, Scott went down to see if there was an intruder. He told them that he had been asleep in his bed. He had no recollection of anything having happened between the time when he hit the mattress, dead tired, around 9:45 p.m., until he was awoken by their noise. If he were the perpetrator, the only explanation he could think of was that he must have gone crazy. The possibility of *non-insane automatism* did not occur to him.

As in the Kenneth Parks case, the examining psychiatrist found no serious mental illness that would account for Scott killing his wife, Yarmila. After administering a battery of tests, a psychologist concluded Scott was normal. A neurologist ruled out seizure disorder. Everyone who knew Scott described him as an even-tempered individual who had been happily married for twenty years. He served as an elder in his church and, with Yarmila, did many good works in their community.

After the medical and psychological experts ruled out all the above explanations for Scott's attack, his sister Laura conducted a computer search to see if she could find any similar situations. Coming across the Kenneth Parks case, she saw that these two killings had much in common. She recalled her brother sleepwalking as a child. Sometimes he did this as an adult, too. For example, shortly before his marriage, when he was twenty years old, Scott was still living at home. Around midnight, when Laura was in the kitchen, he came down in his pyjamas and headed out the back door. From the blank, staring look on his face, she knew he was somnambulating. To prevent him going outside, she placed herself between him and the door. Grabbing her firmly by the shoulders, Scott flung her across the room. His unusual violence startled Laura. It was so completely at odds with his usual waking behavior.

Based on her computer research, Laura suggested to Scott's lawyers that her brother could have killed Yarmila during somnambulism. They agreed with her. The idea that Scott had been sleepwalking had evidently not occurred to the psychiatrist, neurologist, and psychologist who examined him any more than the possibility of parasomnia had entered the minds of the mental health care specialists who examined Oscar. When the idea of parasomnia was proposed to Scott, he resisted that possibility.

Dr. Cartwright, who had served as one of the expert witnesses for Kenneth Parks' legal team, was approached by Scott's lawyers to perform the same sort of service she had done for Ken. Observing that the sleepwalking defense had not seemed plausible to Scott, she attributed his skepticism to the fact that he was a practical-minded engineer, not someone given to 'flights of fantasy.'

Approximately two years after the killing, Scott agreed to his first interview with the media. He explained that initially: "I thought my brain had thrown a rod. And I thought, 'I'm going to the State Hospital, or the prison for life ... ' Sometimes when I think about this, I wonder, 'What kind of Jekyll and Hyde am I? ...At first, I considered the sleepwalking defense bullshit, pure and simple."

Professor Cartwright noted that Scott had performed two aggressive acts. After stabbing Yarmila, he had gone back into his home. He re-emerged later to look at, then roll his wife into the pool. When Scott went to trial, this two-step sequence became a stumbling point for the jury. The defense sleep experts, David Baratz and Mark Pressman, did not believe the facts of the case supported a defense of somnambulism. For example, the literature suggested aggressive sleepwalkers usually remain in a state of confusional arousal for a short period of time, approximately fifteen minutes. In contrast, the sleepwalking defense would have to propose that Scott remained in a state of semiconsciousness for over an hour after his initial attack. Dr. Cartwright agreed she had found no similar cases in the literature but, she said, she also knew "*much about these strange disorders was then and still is unknown*" [italics added]. When cases involve facts that push the envelope of what is known to be possible in parasomnia, sleep experts can honestly disagree on what most likely happened. In other instances that go less beyond current knowledge, such as the Kenneth Parks case, all the sleep specialists for both the prosecution and the defense may agree that the terrible tragedy had been committed during a parasomniac state.

One of the defense sleep experts in Scott's case, Dr. Roger Broughton, admitted to the court that certain facts presented by the prosecution gave him pause about his conclusion that Scott had been sleepwalking. In contrast, Professor Cartwright remained convinced that Scott had committed these awful acts during non-REM sleep. Quickly she became aware that the jury did not share her belief. Sitting back in their chairs, one juror rolled her eyes. Just one member of that group, an elderly black man, leaned forward and followed Dr. Cartwright's testimony closely. The others looked like they had already made up their minds. The prosecutor was sarcastically dismissive toward Dr. Cartwright.

The jurors agreed with the prosecution and their sleep specialists. Scott was sentenced to life imprisonment without chance of parole. After the trial, jurors told reporters that although no motive had been established, the accused must have had "unconscious hostility" toward his wife that drove him to kill her.

Could those jurors be right that Scott might have had unconscious (and even conscious) hostility toward his wife, and might Dr. Cartwright also be correct in her belief that Scott killed his wife during a somnambulistic episode? Might these explanations be complementary rather than mutually exclusive?

Scott had not been sleeping well because of prolonged work stress. To fight his fatigue, he consumed caffeine tablets. He had been assigned a big project that involved developing a new computer chip. Progress on this endeavor was not promising. He wanted to tell management they should abandon it, but feared they would see him as a failure. Pride in his vocational competence constituted a major component of Scott's self image. Shutting down this project would likely cost the company millions of dollars and jeopardize his team of coworkers that looked up to him, causing some of them to lose their jobs.

The evening before the killing, Scott told Yarmila he intended to inform his supervisors the project needed to be terminated. She advised him not to: "Just tell them what they want to hear." Scott was disappointed by his wife's response. Their conversation ended with both of them feeling dissatisfied.

In his July 1, 1999 article in the *Phoenix New Times*, Paul Rubin noted that:

> During cross-examination, Falater continued to blurt unintentionally ironic phrases such as: 'The last nail in the coffin,' referring to a failing project at Motorola. 'Spilling engineer blood,' again about the moribund project. 'In order for Motorola to minimize the blood loss and the money loss ...

Although it is not in keeping with how most sleep experts usually think, I wonder whether those vivid phrases might not only be ironic but also allude to something deeper and more significant. Earlier I referred to the possibility that some parasomniac killers might unconsciously be desperately attempting to reverse their psychic situation. Fearing humiliation, mortification, and psychic annihilation, they may endeavor to radically reverse their predicament, inflicting it on someone else in order to escape a dreadful fate. Terrified that at work his engineer blood might soon be flowing, to be followed no doubt by a final nail being hammered into his coffin, Scott may have been unconsciously inclined to inflict this fate onto someone else. In this hypothetical scenario, he could have imposed this horrid destiny onto whomever was closest at hand. Perhaps parasomniacally unknown to him, this turned out to be his wife. She was the wrong person in the wrong place at the wrong time.

In keeping with this possibility, Scott may have been correct when he told a journalist that: "I thought my brain had thrown a rod." In terms of unconscious defenses and the neurophysiological processes underlying parasomnia, he may have been right. In the courtroom, the prosecutor showed a photo of Yarmila's butchered body on the autopsy table. Only unconsciously might Scott have believed that this image was better than the one he earlier had in mind of his engineer blood being spilled, preparatory to the last nail being hammered into his coffin.

The second issue on Scott's mind before he retired to bed that evening concerned a malfunctioning pool filter motor. Yarmila had asked him to fix it. When he inspected the device, he remembers thinking, "At least I can do this job." Too tired to complete it at the time, he went to bed. Later, Dr. Cartwright reasoned, he got up in his sleep to finish fixing the filter motor in order to restore his self-image as someone who is both a competent engineer and a good husband. Those simple, everyday ideas and dreams often occur during non-REM sleep. When Scott got up, Yarmila may have tried to get him to go back to bed. Oblivious as to whom he was attacking, Scott may have stabbed her for interfering with his drive to repair his battered self esteem by completing this simple task.

Such a dramatic shift from benign activity to aggression has been known to happen when sleepwalkers misperceive harmless gestures as attacks. They feel the appropriate response is to fight back. In these counterattacks, they have no awareness of whom they are harming. They do not recognize faces. To illustrate this non-recognition, consider what one man's wife told Professor Schenck (2005):

> Some nights he would jump out of bed and he would look right at me. His eyes would be open with absolute terror on his face. He would not know who I was. He would say, 'Who are you? What are you doing here?' He would be ready to pounce, just like that. I would just stand still, right where I was, maybe ten feet away from him. I wouldn't dare move. (p. 278)

Even if Scott's drive to repair the pool's filter motor and his self-esteem were extremely important to him, is a brutal, two-step death sentence not far too extreme a punishment to mete out to someone for interfering with his project?

From a common sense perspective, Scott's reaction was way beyond excessive. From the point of view of unconscious processing, however, it may have seemed appropriate. To understand this difference between the conscious and unconscious mind, consider Freud's (1915) thoughts:

> In our unconscious impulses we daily and hourly get rid of anyone who stands in our way, of anyone who has offended or injured us. ...Indeed, our unconscious will murder even for trifles; like the ancient Athenian code of Draco, it knows no other punishment for crime than death. And this has a certain consistency, for every injury to our almighty and autocratic ego is at bottom a crime of *lèse-majesté* [BW: *literally 'injured greatness;' a crime or offense against the sovereign power, especially against the ruler's dignity*]. ...If we are to be judged by our unconscious wishful impulses, we ourselves are, like primaeval man, a gang of murderers. ...Loved ones are on the one hand an inner possession, components of our own ego; but on the other hand they are partly strangers, even enemies. With the exception of only a very few situations, there adheres to the tenderest and most intimate of our love-relations a small portion of hostility which can excite an unconscious death-wish. (p. 297)

In keeping with Freud's findings and cogitations, we can imagine when Scott Falater retired to bed, he may have harbored a death wish toward Yarmila (and authorities at work). These unconscious thoughts and impulses may have contributed to his somnambulistic violence. "Our unconscious will murder even for trifles."

Before introducing the above ideas, Freud wrote: "Our unconscious does not carry out the killing; it merely thinks it and wishes it. But it would be wrong so completely to undervalue this psychical reality as compared with factual reality. It is significant and momentous enough." Generally Freud is correct that the unconscious does not actually murder anyone. However, in parasomniac killing, the unconscious not only thinks and wishes to slay someone but also actually does so. Even as renowned a neurologist and psychoanalyst as Sigmund Freud did not seem aware that such real killings could be conducted by seemingly normal, or even exemplary individuals. In his defense, we can assert that the modern era of research into sleep and its disorders did not commence until after he had died.

Leaving Scott Falater's trial, Professor Cartwright had many questions. She wondered whether the jurors might have been correct in assuming unconscious hostility. Her experience indicated that sleepwalkers tend to over control their basic drives and lack response flexibility when new adaptation is required. Their dogged self-control can reach obsessive-compulsive proportions. In the older legal literature, she knew this personality feature has been remarked upon as characteristic of sleepwalkers.

After Scott's verdict had been handed down, with her interest in dreams, Dr. Cartwright asked him to keep a dream diary. In the resulting large sample, taken over nine years, there were no dreams in which he was physically aggressive with Yarmila. In only one out of the 196 dreams did he attack anyone (because of disparaging remarks a male made against other people). Far more often, he portrayed himself as escaping from attackers. Frequently he hid or sought refuge.

In Scott's dreams, Dr. Cartwright detected a clear change in his conception of Yarmila over time. In the first of three phases (1999 to 2002), Yarmila was seen as a strong, sensible, attractive, loving mate of whom Scott was proud. He was often lost or stuck and she was consistently knowledgeable and supportive. In one striking dream during this period, Scott was given a rifle. He was asked to kill a "dead" deer if it proved dangerous. He did not want to and did not have to because the creature escaped and was reunited with family. Scott and Yarmila were happy to witness this non-violent, miraculous turn of events. Dr. Cartwright described this dream as double wish fulfillment. The dead deer turned out to be alive and rejoined her family. Furthermore, Yarmila was alive and loved her husband.

Scott's dreamwork seemed to conveniently displace his troubled feelings about Yarmila onto an animal. He did not kill that deer (dear). He does not need to follow instructions to kill the dead creature a second time should it prove to be, or be perceived as, posing danger. All these events are in marked contrast to Scott's two killings of Yarmila: stabbing her forty-four times, then drowning her. To top this wishful dream revision off, the deer resurrected and rejoined her family, much as Scott no doubt wished Yarmila would rejoin him.

Of course on a rational level a dead animal could not pose any threat that would need to be responded to with gunfire. In the unconscious, however, things can be very different. A dead deer could represent André Green's (or Winnicott's) emotionally 'dead mother" that does, indeed, pose an enormous threat to psychological wellbeing. Furthermore, dead Yarmila could easily arise from her grave as a ghost to haunt and torment Scott. In the unconscious, no one ever truly dies. Resurrection is always possible.

By displacing his problem onto the deer, Scott's unconscious enabled him to process his tragic domestic situation in a far less disturbing realm, involving an animal victim rather than his wife. In contrast, if he had dreamt all this in relation to the actual tragedy, as often occurs in post-traumatic stress disorder nightmares, he would probably have awoken in a cold sweat. Freud believed such protective concealment was integral to dreaming, designed to insulate the sleeper from intolerable, raw impulses and experience in order to facilitate obtaining much needed, restorative rest.

In contrast to Yarmila's first phase, loving, supportive role, in the middle stage of Scott's dreaming (2002 to 2004), she had opposite qualities: ugly, dominant, reckless, castrating. In the final phase (2005 to 2006), Yarmila went her own way, leaving Scott behind. He was angry at her lack of understanding of his frailty and her lack of support for him.

As Scott worked through his relationship with Yarmila in his dreams, he got increasingly in touch with what the jurors referred to as his probable "unconscious hostility". As Freud observed, however, such unconscious impulses are commonplace, perhaps universal. They do not usually lead to actual murder. Only when neurophysiological complications (including transient ones related to stress, sleep deprivation, drugs, and other such factors) allow access to motility during the sleeping state may this deadly outcome occur.

Like Scott Falater, Oscar, without the concept of possible parasomnia at his disposal, simply stuck to the 'facts' as he recalled them, even though his version of reality was in important respects contradicted by forensic evidence and, in other regards, totally implausible. When 'facts' (e.g., Police Photograph #68) conflicted with what Oscar 'knew' to be true, he denied them in his quest to resolve these contradictions. He insisted police evidence had been manufactured. Otherwise, he admitted, his account would have been rendered untenable by those photographs. He had no way of thinking that his version could have accurately portrayed (subjective) reality whereas the police photograph reflected a different, objective reality.

Just as Kenneth Parks and Scott Falater initially resisted the idea that they could have killed their loved ones in a somnambulistic state, Oscar would likely also have opposed the idea, perhaps quite vigorously, that he could have been anything other than completely alert and fully in possession of all his faculties at all times. The scientific evidence in this chapter suggests that such assertions need to be regarded at less than face value.

Chapter 19

A PLENTITUDE OF PARASOMNIAS

Whosoever saves a single soul is regarded
as though he saved a complete world.
—The Talmud

If anyone saves a life, it shall be as though
he had saved the lives of all mankind.
—The Koran

"The study of sleep teaches us that for all our vast and rapidly increasing knowledge, *we're still babes in the woods*. It was barely 50 years ago that we even learned that such a thing as REM sleep existed, and now we're continuing to uncover 'new' conditions, parasomnias that have likely existed across species since well before the arrival of man" (Schenck, 2007, italics added). It is important to bear in mind the fact that we still have much to learn about parasomnias. Even what we do know may only apply in a substantial number of cases, perhaps even the majority, rather than being true in all cases and in any particular instance.

There are now many reports of people with rapid eye movement sleep behavior disorder dreaming they were performing acceptable or even admirable actions, such as trying to protect loved ones from dangerous intruders, only to wake up and find they were harming, or had even killed their beloved. Complicating this picture, research has shown that more than 10% of people with RBD are unaware of any dreaming associated with their abnormal behaviors. Oscar Pistorius never brought up the possibility that he may have been caught up in a dream enactment the night he killed his girlfriend.

We discussed the possibility that the Blade Runner might have attacked Reeva during rapid eye movement sleep behavior disorder or some other parasomnia, such as dreamwalking or sexsomnia. His uncharacteristic behavior, whether it was aggressive and/or sexual, could have caused his girlfriend to flee to the bathroom, slamming and locking its door behind her. Oscar might have no memory of having acted oddly or inappropriately during these events, or of having been in a dream state.

An example of new variations on sleep disorders that research is gradually uncovering is *parasomnia overlap disorder* (POD). This term, coined by Professor Schenck and his colleagues in a 1997 paper, indicates that one can have not only RBD but also a disorder of arousal such as sleepwalking, confusional arousal, and/or sleep terror—sometimes all in the same night. In fact, "It is not uncommon," Dr. Schenck (2005) writes, "for people to be afflicted with multiple parasomnias" (p. 24). Like RBD, POD has a male predominance (70%) but a lesser one. It has an earlier age of onset. Most cases begin in adolescence, but it can occur at any age. Of the 33 cases Dr. Schenck and his co-workers studied, the mean age was 33.8 (approximately Oscar's age), with a range from 5 to 72 years.

Within the category of arousal disorders, the situation is much more varied than originally believed. Classic descriptions of sleepwalking and night terrors indicated that they occur early in the night, with virtually no self-awareness during episodes. We now know these disorders can occur at any time. It was, and often still is believed that there is no dreaming, or only brief dream fragments without plot, and little or no recall during these events. Professor Schenck (2005) notes that while this picture may be largely true for children and teens, many adults have considerable recall of vivid, lengthy dreams during these episodes. *Some individuals felt completely awake*—until they were awakened.

In another of the seemingly endless parasomniac variations, some people can act out dreams while technically awake. This condition is known as *pseudo-RBD*. A clinic in Barcelona reported on sixteen men who complained of harmful, or potentially dangerous dream-enacting behaviors. Two had assaulted their spouses during sleep. Five fell out of bed. Two suffered lacerations on their faces and arms. All reported dreams similar to what might be expected in RBD, such as being attacked or chased by humans or animals. Polysomnographic study showed that during REM sleep they all had atonia (inability to move) and they also did not have the usual muscle twitching, so they did not have RBD. What they did have was severe obstructive sleep apnea (OSA) and severe obstructive hypopneas. In these conditions, respiratory passages collapse and airflow stops completely (apnea) or partially (hypopnea). Breathing usually halts for ten to thirty seconds but can go on for more than a minute. At these times, the oxygen-deprived brain sounds an alarm (a physiological variation on Freud's psychological night watchman), waking the individual. This arousal jolts the upper airway open, permitting proper airflow. The person then goes back to sleep. People can wake up a hundred times per night, or even per hour. To qualify for this diagnosis, one must stop breathing for at least ten seconds, a minimum of five times per hour, throughout the night. Most times, the person is not aware of these sleep disruptive episodes. Often their bed partner observes choking, gasping, or lapses in breathing. Far from being rare, OSA is the most common reason people are referred to sleep clinics.

The Spanish men averaged more than one respiratory disturbance per minute. When doctors examined the videotaped polysomnographs, they witnessed kicking, gesturing, arm raising, shouting, and talking. These behaviors always coincided with an arousal from REM or NREM sleep triggered by apnea. Every time these patients dream-enacted, they had just been aroused by the need for oxygen. These behaviors did not arise without that trigger. Technically they are 'awake' while enacting dreams. Since OSA is common and most frequent and severe during REM sleep, the time when RBD emerges, pseudo-RBD parasomnia may be considerably more prevalent than currently recognized.

Bearing the above complexities of sleep and dreaming in mind, on Saint Valentine's Day 2013, Oscar Pistorius may have had a normal dream of convenience and may have suffered one or more parasomnias such as nightmare, pavor nocturnus, sexsomnia, rapid eye movement sleep behavior disorder, or dreamwalking. He could have no awareness or memory of having experienced any abnormality related to disordered sleep, wakefulness, or dreaming. He could simply think he had been trying to protect himself and Reeva even though, as Judge Masipa and Bail Magistrate Nair emphasized, there were glaring, important aspects of that narrative that made absolutely no sense.

Chapter 20

SENTENCING OSCAR ONCE, TWICE, THREE, ...

There are more things in heaven and earth, Horatio, than are dreamt of in your philosophy [science].
—Shakespeare, *Hamlet*

On September 12, 2014 Oscar Leonard Carl Pistorius was found guilty of culpable homicide (manslaughter) and of an earlier charge, reckless endangerment, related to accidentally discharging a friend's firearm in a restaurant. Judge Masipa ruled that Oscar was *not guilty* of two other charges: illegal possession of ammunition and firing a firearm through a car's sunroof. The state had thrown the book at the Blade Runner in terms of offences he may have committed. A month later, on October 21, 2014 Judge Masipa handed him a five-year prison sentence for the Saint Valentine's Day tragedy and a concurrent three-year suspended sentence for the reckless endangerment conviction.

Oscar's brother, Carl, told a South African weekly that his sibling did not receive any special privileges in prison. He was permitted one hour of daily outdoor exercise and another hour in the weight room. Utilizing his expertise in athletics and physical training for the other inmates' benefit, he counseled them in the hospital wing about exercise. He also wanted to initiate a basketball program.

Eight months later (June 2015), Oscar was recommended for early release. In South African, one is eligible to leave prison under correctional supervision after serving a sixth of one's sentence. Based on good behavior and the fact that he was not considered a danger to the community, Oscar's discharge to house arrest was announced for August 21. He was expected to perform community service and would not be able to return to official athletic competition until his full five years had been served.

Two days before Oscar was to leave the Pretoria prison, his departure was blocked by the Justice Minister who deemed the parole board's decision "premature." Legal experts thought this reversal was likely due to political pressure and also because this leniency had implications for other cases. Two months later, Oscar was released to serve the remainder of his sentence at his uncle's home.

The State's Appeal

Less than a month after Oscar's initial sentencing, the prosecutors applied to the sentencing judge for permission to challenge the homicide verdict. They claimed the five-year term was "shockingly light, inappropriate and would not have been imposed by any reasonable court." Judge Masipa ruled that the prosecution could appeal her acquitting Oscar of premeditated murder, but not his sentence.

The Supreme Court of Appeal heard the State's case eleven months later, on November 3, 2015. The prosecution claimed Judge Masipa had made an error in concluding Oscar had not foreseen that by firing four shots he would likely kill whoever was behind the door.

Before delivering the Supreme Court's verdict, Judge Eric Leach stated:

> This case involves a human tragedy of Shake-
> spearean proportions: a young man overcomes

huge physical disabilities to reach Olympian heights as an athlete; in doing so he becomes an international celebrity; he meets a young woman of great natural beauty and a successful model; romance blossoms; and then, ironically on Valentine's Day, all is destroyed when he takes her life.

Despite this epic "human tragedy of Shakespearean proportions," the Supreme Court agreed with the prosecution. Overturning the homicide conviction, they judged Oscar guilty of murder with "indirect intent." The case was referred back to Judge Masipa for a second sentencing. The Supreme Court agreed with the lower court that Oscar had:

been a very poor witness. His version varied substantially. At the outset he stated that he had fired the four shots "before I knew it" and at a time when he was not sure if there was somebody in the toilet. This soon changed to a version that he had fired as he believed that whoever was in the toilet was going to come out to attack him. He later changed this to say that he had never intended to shoot at all; that he had not fired at the door on purpose and that he had not wanted to shoot at any intruder coming out of the toilet. In the light of these contradictions, one really does not know what his explanation is for having fired the fatal shots.

From the scientific study of sleep, dreaming, and parasomnia, and investigations of the psychology of perception, narrative construction, and memory under conditions of extreme fear, one would hardly expect Oscar to have been able to provide a comprehensive, cohesive, consistent account that would be fully satisfactory in all particulars to all listeners, or even to himself, as indicated in his post-trial statement on ITV: "How could this possibly have happened?" When one has been under extreme stress, not to mention simultaneously, or oscillatingly, being in states of nightmare, sleep terror, dream enactment, and confusional arousal, there are likely to be gaps, distortions, contradictions, and so forth in one's report.

Understanding that Oscar may have not been in a calm state of mind, Judge Leach stated:

> Although he may have been anxious, it is inconceivable that a *rational person* [BW: italics added] could have believed he was entitled to fire at this person with a heavy-calibre firearm, without taking even that most elementary precaution of firing a warning shot.

The crucial term in Judge Leach's statement is: "a rational person." If, as I believe, Oscar was not rational at the moment in question, that is if he had been in a hyperaroused state of altered consciousness, then the prosecution's argument pertaining to what a rational person would or should do, and the Supreme Court of Appeal's endorsement of that position, would not be relevant. If the Supreme Court had been presented with the idea that Oscar was not a rational person during that tragedy but, rather, was in a complex state involving a disorder of sleep, dreaming, arousal, and consciousness, I do not think they would have found him guilty of culpable homicide, let alone murder. He, like Kenneth Parks and many others who did very bad things while in parasomniac states, would have been acquitted and sentenced to appropriate treatment to minimize or eliminate the chance of any future, violent, parasomniac events.

The Defense's Appeal

Following the Supreme Court's decision, Oscar continued under house arrest pending his own appeal to the

Constitutional Court, South Africa's highest judicial body – the court of last resort. On March 3, 2016 his right to that appeal was denied because the Court believed it had no reasonable chance of success. He would have to appear again in Judge Masipa's chambers on June 13, 2016 to begin a five-day re-sentencing hearing for his murder conviction.

Might Oscar's appeal to the Constitutional Court have been treated differently if his defense team had been able to bring forth significant *new* material that had not been considered in his previous trials? If they had been able to present the case that Oscar, like Kenneth Parks and others, killed during an altered state of consciousness (parasomnia)? If they had been able to demonstrate that this new, scientific understanding finally enabled the Court to account for *all the evidence*, providing scientifically credible comprehension of all the otherwise *glaring gaps* in the Court's (and everyone else's) understanding of this tragic case? I believe the answer is yes. Despite it being politically incorrect in some quarters to contemplate alternative explanations in this case, even if they are scientifically sound, only these elucidations can enable us to meet the fundamental legal standard of accounting for all the evidence.

Different Worlds of Justice

Depending on where one lives, the South African justice system could seem admirable and/or peculiar. In the USA, it would seem odd that Oscar never faced a jury of his peers. What would probably baffle most Americans even more would be the Courts' belief that his terror that intruders were about to harm him and Reeva was no excuse for not having called the police, or fleeing, or firing a warning shot. In contrast, in the USA, the right to bear arms and to defend oneself from perceived threats, especially in one's home, is widely endorsed as an almost sacred, constitutionally protected right. To most U.S. citizens, the idea that Oscar believed his residence had been invaded and that he and

Reeva were in imminent danger would be considered sufficient to justify his shooting.

While some might feel South African Courts lean too far in one direction with respect to rights to aggressive self-defence, others would believe the American justice system goes too far the other way. Consider the case of Trayvon Martin, the seventeen-year-old African-American teenager who was fatally shot by George Zimmerman, a neighborhood watch volunteer, in Sanford, Florida. On February 26, 2012, Trayvon was returning to his father's home from a convenience store. Having just purchased some candy and a watermelon drink, he was chatting on his cellphone with his girlfriend. As he passed through a neighborhood that had been victimized by several robberies that year, George spotted him and called the police to report 'suspicious behavior'. Zimmerman was told to not take any action, to wait for the police. Moments later, there was an altercation during which George shot Trayvon to death. Zimmerman was not charged at the time of the shooting. Police said there was no evidence to refute his self-defense claim.

Many people vehemently disagreed with the police. Rallies and marches sprung up across the nation. A Change. org petition calling for full investigation and prosecution garnered over two million signatures—the most ever in that website's history. Trayvon's killing became the first story that year to be featured more than the Presidential race. Passionate debate about racial profiling and stand your ground laws ensued.

Florida had been the first state to pass a law allowing individuals who feel threatened to stand their ground. Governor Rick Scott established a task force to review and make recommendations about that statute. Trayvon's parents and members of the Second Chance on Shoot First campaign delivered a petition with three hundred and forty thousand signatures to that Citizen Safety and Protection task force, asking for changes to that law. A National Rifle Association lobbyist who had helped write that legislation, insisted there was nothing wrong with it. Ultimately the task force recommended against repealing the statute, saying Florida's residents had a right to defend themselves with deadly force without a duty to retreat if they feel threatened. With respect to self-defense law, Oscar lived in the wrong country. In the U.S.A., he would probably have been found not guilty. He would have proceeded to participate in the 2016 Rio de Janeiro Olympics. In South Africa, in contrast, even after being released for good behavior to serve the remainder of his sentence at his uncle's home, he was forbidden from participating in any athletic competitions until he had served his full sentence. His career, finances, economic prospects—basically his whole life—was ruined.

Despite the police belief that Zimmerman could not be arrested, he was eventually charged and tried. In July 2013, a jury agreed with the original police assessment. They acquitted him of second-degree murder and manslaughter. Four days later, a group calling themselves the Dream Defenders began a sit-in at the State Capitol. They wanted to force a special session on Florida's stand your ground law. Another group of Trayvon supporters walked for six days from Jacksonville to Sanford to protest that statute. In Los Angeles, a garden at Crenshaw High School was dedicated to Trayvon and a march was held to teach students how to express their First Amendment rights while *standing their ground* for youth civil rights.

Six days after Zimmerman's acquittal, President Obama thoughtfully opined: "It would be useful for us to examine some state and local laws to see ...if they are designed in such a way that they may encourage the kinds of altercations and confrontations and tragedies that we saw in the Florida case, rather than defuse potential altercations." He discussed his experiences as an African-American man and the history of racial disparities in how laws are applied to African-Americans, in everything from the death penalty to drug laws. Those experiences have impacted how African-Americans interpret what happened that night and in the ensuing couple of years leading up to Zimmerman's acquittal. "Trayvon Martin could have been me thirty-five years ago," Obama shared somberly.

Like Oscar, Trayvon may have been born in the wrong country regarding self-defense legislation. In South Africa, Zimmerman's behavior would have been viewed differently. He would likely have been tried for murder and found guilty.

Second Sentencing

Oscar's second sentencing hearing – for murder rather than manslaughter—began on Monday June 13, 2016, concluding on Friday. Reeva's father testified on the trauma his family suffered. Although he and his wife had expressed forgiveness because of their Christian beliefs, Mr. Steenkamp insisted Oscar "must pay". Whereas previously Reeva's parents had refused to speak with Oz, Mr. Steenkamp said he would like to talk with him some day. Defense lawyer Barry Roux said there was nothing Oscar would like more.

The final witness, Reeva's cousin and close friend, Kim Martin, claimed Oz gave many versions of the shooting and never properly apologized. "We just want the truth," she pleaded. Similarly in closing argument, prosecutor Nel claimed Oscar had never shown remorse since he had never given an honest explanation for why he fired. Kim's understandable longing for the truth about her cousin's death would have to wait until new light could be thrown on what happened. Without knowledge of sleep, dreaming, altered consciousness, and parasomnia, she would be doomed to dwell forever in dark distress about this matter. With this scientific perspective, she might at last have the truth for which she yearns.

Without these crucial scientific insights, Oscar, too, would be left perplexed, lamenting: "I always think 'How did this possibly happen?' How could this have happened?" His queries will forever plague him (and others) unless he becomes more familiar with relevant findings from the science of sleep and dreaming, and their disorders.

"Is an intruder's life not important?" prosecutor Nel asked. "Did he think of that life? He did not." From the perspective of research in sleep, dreaming, and parasomnia, Oscar would have been *unable* to think very much about the value of an intruder's life if he were in a state of dream enactment or confusional arousal when he fired. In a parasomniac, kill or be killed frame of mind, he would only be able to think of taking immediate action to protect himself and Reeva. More complex cognition involving empathic evaluation of the pros and cons of diverse possible scenarios is not feasible in a paranoid-schizoid state of confusional hyperarousal.

Arguing for a lenient sentence, Oscar's defense attorney, Barry Roux, emphasized that at the time of the shooting Oscar was fearful, vulnerable, and trying to protect his girlfriend. He would pay for this killing for the rest of his life because he is a "broken man" in constant pain, financially ruined, filled with self-loathing, vilified by the public, his once stellar career now destroyed.

Clinical psychologist Professor Jonathan Scholtz evaluated Oscar in 2014 during his trial and in May 2016 prior to the second sentencing hearing. He testified that Oscar's mental state had deteriorated over the last two years. Struggling with depression and posttraumatic stress disorder, he should be hospitalized rather than jailed, Dr. Scholtz averred.

On July 6, 2016 Judge Masipa re-sentenced Oscar to serve six more years. The year that he had already served, followed by seven months' house arrest, was not subtracted from this new sentence. Defense lawyers had asked that he be given no further jail time. They argued that he should, instead, do charity work with children, something he had done to good effect in the past. At the opposite end of the legal spectrum, the prosecution wanted at least the usual minimum fifteen years' mandatory imprisonment required in cases where there are no mitigating circumstances. Judge Masipa believed there were extenuating factors. I, of course, believe that on top of the substantial and compelling factors she considered, there was another, even greater mitigating variable: parasomnia.

Reactions to Oscar's Second Sentence

The day after Oscar's second sentencing, an article by Ranjeni Munusamy appeared in *The Guardian (African Network)* entitled, "Oscar Pistorius Sentence: An Homage to Celebrity and White Privilege." Ranjeni spoke for a significant sector of the public vehemently opposed to leniency. The words immediately following her provocative title, just prior to the text, elaborated her perspective: "The laughable six-year jail term is a reminder of how inequality continues to penetrate the South African justice system." Excerpts from her article will convey the anger many still held three and a half years after that dreadful night.

According to Munusamy, Oscar felt sorry for himself for being burdened with the process of justice. At his second sentencing, Judge Masipa got another chance to "massage Pistorius's privilege." The magistrate decided there were substantial and compelling circumstances permitting her to deviate from the required 15-year minimum sentence for murder.

> Of course there were exceptional circum-
> stances...It was about society indulging and cel-
> ebrating him...In Pistorius's charmed life...the
> justice system should have...trundled off to hold
> lesser mortals accountable for their actions...
> We simply cannot have him shut away when he
> could be helping the "less fortunate" among us.
> "If I was afforded the opportunity of redemp-

tion, I would like to help the less fortunate like I had in my past…I would like to believe that if Reeva could look down upon me that she would want me to live that life."

The "less fortunate" have no say in this and neither does Steenkamp. Her family, who suffered unimaginable trauma and grief, have also been left without justice for her murder.

Masipa's primary concern…was the "broken man" in the dock. "The life of the accused will never be the same…He is a fallen hero who has lost his career and been ruined financially…"

Masipa said the continuing misperception that Pistorius had intentionally killed Steenkamp was something the court had a duty to correct to "prevent unjustified outrage from the public"… Unjustified? Really? What is the appropriate response to murder?…

This was also not a case of gender violence, Masipa said.…Masipa is convinced there was no argument between the couple that night—but it does not mean the rest of us will. We also did not fall for Pistorius's whimpering as evidence of "genuine remorse", which Masipa found to be a mitigating factor for a light sentence.

The Pistorius case was sickening from the very beginning and this sentence, if left unchallenged, sets a dangerous precedent for exceptionalism… We are reminded once again of how the justice system can be used as a white man's plaything.

An earlier version of Munusamy's article appeared in The Daily Maverick, a South African website where she is an Associate Editor.

Like Munusamy, Dukes Masanabo, a South African sports official who had hoped Pistorius would be sentenced to 10-12 years, not six, said, "The law didn't take its course." The sentence is too light, he claimed, because it was almost the same as Oscar had received for his earlier conviction. Some campaigners for women's rights, like Jacqui Mofokeng of the African National Congress Women's League, expressed outrage at what she and her group perceived to be excessive lenience: "The judgment is an insult to women. It sends the wrong message."

Rage at Oscar had been present in many quarters since the initial news of the tragedy. On October 14, 2014 a man who called himself 'Mr. Noose' arrived at North Gauteng High Court in Pretoria, South Africa, where the Blade Runner was about to be sentenced for culpable homicide. Waving a hangman's noose he had fashioned from a length of rope, he declared that he wanted to see justice delivered for crimes against women. Representing the sentiment of many others, it was clear what penalty Mr. Noose felt the Blade Runner deserved.

These angry commentators on Oscar Pistorius' crime and sentencing might have had a different opinion if they had been aware of the possibility that the dreaming and parasomnia hypotheses could provide the necessary key for unlocking all the fundamental mysteries permeating this tragic case.

Behind Bars Again

Not long after Oscar began serving his sentence for murder, Jade Wilsons reported on a South African website that the Blade Runner had been hospitalized after falling off his upper bunk. Haunted by Reeva, Oscar had thrown himself off his bed, her headline read. His cellmate shared: "The fall was intense. It was as if he was thrown down. I heard his bones crack." He seemed to have been fighting with a ghost, this man averred. Cellmates and prison officials reportedly said that ever since arriving, Oscar had gotten no sleep. He was seeing dead people and pleading with Reeva to stop tormenting him.

That article, to the extent that it is accurate, suggests to me that Oscar continued to suffer from parasomnia. While in bed, whatever he might have been dreaming, his brain's access to motility was not shut off. Wilson's description that he had thrown himself off his bed is commonplace in rapid eye movement sleep behavior disorder. Spouses frequently report their partners catapulting out of bed in great fear, hurling themselves into walls, dressers, and other objects, often injuring themselves and breaking objects into which they crash.

A Second Prosecution Appeal?

South African prosecutors were quick to say they would appeal Oscar 's new six-year prison sentence, deeming it "shockingly too lenient" for murder. Six years was, the National Prosecuting Authority declared, "disproportionate to the crime." It could bring the justice system into "disrepute."

On August 26, 2016 Judge Masipa disagreed with the state's argument that Supreme Court judges would find she had treated Oscar too kindly. State prosecutor Nel argued that she had shown "maudlin sympathy" for the Blade Runner's disability and anxiety disorder. Oscar's lawyer said his client had suffered enough. After hearing all these contentions and counter-contentions, Judge Masipa concluded: "I am not persuaded that there are reasonable prospects ...that another court would find differently." The State would have to petition the Supreme Court of Appeal if they hoped to overturn Judge Masipa's decision.

Three weeks later, in the September 15, 2016 issue of The Sun, a British newspaper, South Africa's National Prosecution Authority was quoted as saying it will indeed file papers petitioning the Supreme Court of Appeal for leave to challenge Oscar's second sentencing. A source who knows Oscar and his family well was cited as saying: "Nel will never let this matter rest, he has a point to prove and he is just going to go on and on until he feels he makes it. ... He has lost his sense of perspective, he is no longer acting in a dispassionate way, it is clearly a personal vendetta against Oscar. But we think it could actually backfire against the state now. The Supreme Court of Appeal judges won't do anything with the sentence to make it longer, they could actually make it shorter and Oscar could be out sooner. We feel relaxed about it, justice will take its course." This second plea to the Supreme Court of Appeal was scheduled to occur on November 3, 2017.

The State's Second Appeal

On November 3, 2017, prosecuting attorney Andrea Johnson launched her argument to the Supreme Court of Appeal for Oscar to be given a much harsher sentence. Justice Ronnie Bosielo led the five-judge panel. Ms. Johnson asked the court to grant leave to appeal and to deliver a verdict on the appeal itself.

The question of why Oscar had fired four shots at the toilet door, behind which Reeva was hiding, once again featured prominently during that day's appeal. Advocate Barry Roux, acting for Oscar, was grilled by several of the judges, who asked repeatedly why the Blade Runner had fired so many shots into the toilet cubicle. "To fire four shots into the door and there is no way out of the toilet, is critical," Justice Pieter Meyer said. Justices Bosielo and Willie Seriti said they had read the record of the proceedings and were still in the dark about why Oscar had fired those shots. The matter of multiple shots has been explored in this book. For me it is the least of the many mysteries in this case that Bail Magistrate Nair and Judge Masipa identified. Nonetheless, in the future, judges might find the ideas in this book helpful in understanding this issue that has preoccupied and perplexed them for so long.

On that day of the Prosecution's second appeal, Justice Bosielo seemed supportive of Judge Masipa's rulings. Raising his voice, he declared that Oscar had already apologized enough, and that the Steenkamps had accepted. Andrea Johnson responded that Oscar could have done more. Feeling sorry for oneself is not remorse, she insisted. "Genuine remorse is missing—namely a reason from the respondent for firing the four fatal shots. One cannot say his regret absolves him from the crime."

Throughout the hearing, Andrea Johnson continued to press her point: "His evidence was so contradictory that one simply does not know its true nature. ...We still do not have a true explanation as to why he had shot her." She referred to the remarks of the Supreme Court of Appeal when it had earlier overturned the lower court's culpable homicide verdict, changing it to murder. The justices at the time said: "He never offered a reasonable explanation." Justice Meyer had asked, "Why did he not then take the stand and explain what happened? Why did he not explain the four shots?"

According to the dream enactment hypothesis, Oscar could not provide an explanation that accounted for all the anomalies because he carried out these actions in a dramatically altered state of consciousness. Only a consideration of parasomnia can finally provide a plausible answer to these otherwise never-ending questions.

One judge stated that the Supreme Court of Appeal did not like to meddle with decisions made by lower courts. Right to the end of that day Prosecutor Andrea Johnston argued that Oscar had not told the Pretoria High Court why he shot Reeva. "He should have taken the court into his confidence and said, 'This is why I did it.' With nothing more, there is no gut-wrenching remorse." There was a lack of an admission in terms of acknowledging wrongdoing, Ms. Johnson declared. At that point, Justice Bosielo cut her off saying, "Don't spoil the good point you made." He swiftly ended the hearing, reserving judgment for a future date.

Third Sentencing

Whereas the Supreme Court of Appeal justices seemed to have sympathy for both Judge Masipa and Oscar, when they returned to give their opinion on November 24, 2017, they were, to the surprise of some observers, now fully on board with the Prosecution's position. They did not agree with Judge Masipa that there were any extenuating circumstances that could possibly justify giving the Blade Runner less than the usual minimum 15-year sentence. Now fully siding with the Prosecution, Justice Seriti censured Oscar, saying his apology to the deceased's family during the hearing did "not demonstrate any genuine remorse on his part" and that he "does not appreciate the gravity of his actions. ...I find it difficult on the evidence to accept that the respondent is genuine remorseful. ...[He] has failed to explain why he fired the fatal shots. [He] failed to take the court fully into his confidence. ...To my mind (his) attempt to apologise to the deceased's family does not demonstrate any genuine remorse on his part. ...It is clear that [he] is unable to appreciate the crime he has committed."

The Supreme Court of Appeal proceeded to hand Oscar a fifteen-year sentence, with one and a half years off for time already served. The earliest he would be eligible for parole would be in the year 2023. Pistorius' brother, Carl, responded to this third sentencing on Twitter with three words: "Shattered. Heartbroken. Gutted."

Continuing Appeal

South African media reported that Oscar's lawyers have just one avenue left to them if they want to challenge the new, lengthened sentence handed down by the Supreme Court of Appeal. Their sole remaining option is to appeal this extended prison term to the Constitutional Court. Oscar had already failed with an appeal to them in the previous year when he attempted to challenge his murder conviction.

"I don't think it's over. He has one more option," said lawyer Ulrich Roux, who is not linked to the Pistorius defence. "All the same, there are few grounds of success in this venture. It is pretty much the end of the road for Pistorius." Lawyer Zola Majavu declared similarly that the Constitutional Court was unlikely to agree to hear the case. "In my view, that will be a very tall order. It is pretty much the end of the road for Pistorius." Those unpromising predictions are, of course, all totally transformed when we consider the penetrating insights provided by the scientific study of sleep, dreams, and their disorders. Some courts will permit an appeal if it can be shown that there was scientific evidence available at the time of the trial that was not used by the defense team. That this was the case is clearly the position of this book.

On December 18, 2017 Oscar's legal team presented papers to the Constitutional Court challenging his increased sentence. They argued that the Supreme Court of Appeal had disregarded material findings of the trial court that showed "compelling circumstances justifying a departure from the prescribed minimum sentence." Disregarding these findings of fact undermined Oscar's constitutional right to a fair trial. Their argument relates to the Appeal Court's position on whether substantial and compelling circumstances exist to justify a prison term shorter than the prescribed minimum. The High Court found such reasons did exist, but that finding was rejected by the Appeal Court. The Blade Runner's legal team wants to argue that it is impermissible for the Appeal Court to ignore the considerations of the High Court and that doing so amounts to a breach of the accused's constitutional right to a fair trial. It is understood that the State will oppose this appeal.

Oscar has not done well in the State's two appeals of his conviction and sentence. In the first of those petitions, his conviction was increased from culpable homicide to murder. Oscar's proposal to appeal that decision to the Constitutional Court was rejected on the grounds that it had little if any chance of success. In the State's second petition, his sentence was increased from six to fifteen years. With this series of judgements against him, it does not seem likely that he has much chance of success with the latest application for appeal now being processed. In the event that he does receive a favourable ruling from the Constitutional Court, it would only reduce his prison sentence to somewhere between six and fifteen years. If, however, he were to argue on the basis of this book that scientific evidence was available at the time of his trial that was not used by his defense team, then his conviction could be entirely removed. He would then be seen not as a vile person or monster but rather as an heroic and tragic figure.

Chapter 21

CLOSING ARGUMENT

*The deed does not make a man guilty
unless his mind is guilty.*

—Saint Augustine

In contrast to Saint Augustine's nuanced philosophy, early English law embodied a principle that made people responsible for their conduct no matter what may have been their intentions or motives. Christianity fostered a move away from that simple, rigid notion of culpability. From this more evolved perspective, we can pose the question: Did Oscar have a guilty mind?

A Plea for the Courts to Consider a Scientific Perspective

Ladies and Gentlemen and other distinguished members of the World Court of Public Opinion, thank you so much for having joined me for the purpose of re-viewing this highly enigmatic tragedy. Over the last many pages, we paid particular attention to the several crucial matters that so puzzled Bail Magistrate Nair and Judge Masipa. We are especially indebted to the Judge for having continued to highlight in her Judgment the numerous important unsolved mysteries on which I have focused.

Before pronouncing her verdict, Judge Masipa emphasized: "What must be borne in mind however, is that the conclusion which is reached, whether it be to convict or to acquit must account for *all the evidence*" (italics added). Bluntly, bravely, and wisely, she acknowledged that: "There are indeed a number of aspects in the case which do not make sense." The Judge specified four features that were especially puzzling. These incomprehensible matters had also perplexed Bail Magistrate Nair many months before. Not being experts in the psychology of sleep and dreaming and their aberrations, they could only note, but not begin to comprehend these profound enigmas. Lacking the conceptual base that only the psychology, neurophysiology, and pathology of sleep, dreaming, and consciousness can provide, they could not reach an ideal or even adequate verdict. It was not possible for them to account for all the evidence. Without this specialized scientific knowledge, they struggled to do the best they could with the ideas and facts they had. Like the famous statue of blindfolded Lady Justice with her balancing scales, they, too, were operating in the dark.

We now have the powerful scientific concepts that enable us, finally, to fully account for the totality of evidence in this case – something the court was unable to do. It is now possible for us to determine, in accordance with another revered legal standard, whether Oscar is guilty 'beyond a reasonable doubt.' A murder conviction and, ideally, any judgment should meet this criterion. Although there is no doubt that Oscar killed Reeva, from the valuable perspective provided by extensive research into disorders of sleep and dreaming (parasomnia), I submit that there are compelling reasons to seriously doubt that Oscar Pistorius was criminally responsible for that tragic death.

These many matters that so baffled everyone who seriously examined the events of February 14, 2013 all become completely comprehensible when viewed through the lenses provided by the science of sleep, dreaming, and their disorders. Re-viewing those numerous enigmatic issues from this scientific perspective, one might say, metaphorically speaking, that the wrong man was brought to court. Authorities seized the individual that the world had long admired until their profound respect was eclipsed by the dark events of that Saint Valentine's Day. The killer we needed to examine was the one who, I submit, was not in a rational frame of mind but, rather, was in a dissociated state of dream enactment during this tragic event. A wall of parasomnia divides these two Oscars from each other. The one we have long known and esteemed, then saw in court in an emotionally overwhelmed state, was not the hyperaroused person who, in an altered state of consciousness, ended his lover's life.

The ordinary, rational Oscar would, of course, have checked with his girlfriend to ascertain whether she had heard a sound coming from the bathroom. With his previous girlfriend, Samantha Taylor, he always asked whether she, too, had heard any noise that he had perceived. Oscar would have told Reeva he was going to go down the hallway, with his loaded gun, to investigate what might be going on in the bathroom. Indeed, he claimed he did: "Just as I left my bed, I whispered for Reeva to get down and phone the police." If he had been in a rational frame of mind, he would, of course, have made sure she was actually in the bed, and he would have confirmed with her that she had heard what he was saying to her. Reeva would, of course, have responded to him at all those points. If she did not, he would, of course, have repeated himself until she did respond, or until he realized she was not there. Later, Reeva would have replied to Oscar's repetitive shouting at her and 'the burglars'. From the toilet stall, she would obviously have told him: to calm down; relax; it was just she in there. She would have responded to her lover in all these ways—if she had heard him, if his shouts had not just occurred in his dream. And, of course, Oscar would have heard and heeded Reeva desperately calling to him, telling him to put away his gun – if he had not been in an altered state of consciousness, in a state of dream enactment in which he could not hear her and respond appropriately. All these happenings that made no sense before and throughout the judicial proceedings make perfect sense when regarded from the perspective of parasomnia.

Reeva, her family, relatives, and friends have suffered enormously. So has the normal, admirable, waking Oscar and his family and friends. In television broadcasts and newspaper photographs, the world witnessed the formerly idolized Blade Runner repeatedly retching and drooling into a green plastic bucket provided in the court for that purpose in recognition of the fact that he was in an overwhelmed psychophysiological state of severe distress. The Supreme Court of Appeal rightly intoned that this case constitutes a tragedy of Shakespearian proportions. As Professor Scholtz testified, this admired Olympian was now a broken man. His mental state had deteriorated dramatically over the two years leading up to his second sentencing. Struggling with anxiety, depression, and posttraumatic stress disorder, he should, in that distinguished psychologist's opinion, be hospitalized, not jailed.

Around August 7, 2016, Oscar was taken from prison to a hospital after sustaining wrist injuries. Some said he had cut his wrists in a suicide attempt. Others claimed he had incurred these injuries when falling out of his bunk bed. In any case, his suffering obviously continues.

It seems unlikely or even impossible that Oscar and Reeva would have had to endure such tragic fates had it not been for parasomnia. Their future had looked so bright. Then the lights went out, catapulting them into a horrid dark drama. In view of the above considerations, ladies and gentlemen of the Court of World Opinion, please open your minds to the idea and evidence that Oscar should now be seen in light of precious knowledge obtained from the scientific study of sleep, dreaming, and their disorders. Only after such a careful re-view will we be able to say we have meticulously examined and accounted for all the evidence. It will then be possible to assert that justice has been achieved 'beyond a reasonable doubt'. In contrast, in light of the scientific evidence provided in this book, the very partial accounting for the facts of February 14, 2013 that we otherwise have amounts to justice denied. It may please us to think that something awful happened and that someone has been blamed and punished for that terrible event, but that does not constitute justice.

Reconciliation

The last interview Mr. and Mrs. Steenkamp granted before Oscar's trial was to *The Mail on Sunday*. June Steenkamp was admirably generous. "Whatever the court decides at the end of his trial, I will be ready to forgive him. I know many people in my position would want to see him dead or badly punished. But I believe in faith and justice and I don't have any hatred or revenge in my heart. That's not my way. I would rather pray for him and pray that my family can get through this terrible time. I want to look at Oscar, really look him in the eyes, and see for myself the truth about what he did to Reeva. ...That is my obsession: the truth about why Oscar did what he did that night."

Later, in an interview with *The Guardian* on November 1, 2014, Mrs. Steenkamp discussed Oscar's trial in relation to the book she had written. She reiterated her conviction that: "There's a missing piece. This is not the whole story. I just wish he could have stood up and said exactly what happened." June Steenkamp's profound intuition that the story Oscar told, the narrative the Court believed, was severely lacking is undoubtedly correct. I am convinced Oscar was unable, and still is unable, to provide a more comprehensive, convincing narrative because he was in a parasomniac state of mind— not functioning in an intact cognitive manner—at the time of the tragic killing. There is indeed a missing piece, but Oscar himself does not know what it is due to having been in an altered state of consciousness. If "he could have stood up and said exactly what happened," he probably would have. That is why on British television, after having been found guilty, and lacking knowledge of sleep, dreams, and their disorders, he could only say: "I look back and I think, I always think, 'How did this possibly happen? How could this have happened?' "

The serious look into Oscar's mind and brain that this book provides may be helpful to Mrs. Steenkamp and others who long to peer into the Blade Runner's psyche to find the truth about what transpired that awful night. The tragic loss of Reeva will, of course, continue to profoundly affect her family, friends, and Oscar and his family and friends, and the wider society in South Africa and beyond. Hopefully the fuller truth facilitated by science will help set all those individuals and communities free from the immense shock, confusion, and suffering they have endured.

June Steenkamp acknowledged to *The Guardian* that Oscar had "asked if he could see us, but at that stage we weren't ready to speak to him. What can he say? Sorry is not enough. What can he say and what would we want to talk to him about? I don't know. But one day that confrontation will come. Altercation? Maybe. Violence? No, I don't think so. But that day has to come." The scientific dreaming and parasomnia perspective should enable Reeva's parents and Oscar to one day soon have a very different conversation. Rather than angry confrontation, their newly scientifically informed dialogue could instead become a healing communion.

Rest in peace, sweet Reeva. Now somewhat older and wiser Oscar, may you also come to increasingly rest in peace. May the ideas in this book help all who care about these two individuals and their families and friends to more easily repose, realizing the events of Saint Valentine's Day 2013 were almost certainly a horrific tragedy, not a heinous crime.

**To err is human,
to comprehend and forgive divine.**

About the Author

B rent Willock earned his doctorate in clinical psychology from the University of Michigan. After several years on staff in the Department of Psychiatry at the University of Michigan Medical Center, he relocated to Toronto to become Chief Psychologist at the university-affiliated C.M. Hincks Treatment Center. He was Adjunct Faculty, York University, Associate Faculty Member, School of Graduate Studies, University of Toronto, and taught at the Ontario Institute for Studies in Education.

Dr. Willock is the founding President of the local chapter of the American Psychological Association's Division of Psychoanalysis, and of the Toronto Institute & Society for Contemporary Psychoanalysis. He has contributed many chapters to books, published in prominent journals, and serves on the editorial boards for several journals and book series. For the Washington Psychoanalytic Foundation's New Directions in Psychoanalytic Thinking Program, he is a Writing Mentor. He is author of Comparative-Integrative Psychoanalysis (finalist, Goethe Award), First Editor of Understanding and Coping with Failure; Psychoanalytic

Perspectives on Identity and Difference; Psychoanalytic Perspectives on Passion; On Deaths and Endings (Gradiva Award), Taboo or Not Taboo? (Goethe Award), Loneliness and Longing (Goethe Award).

Dr. Willock serves on the Board of the Canadian Institute for Child & Adolescent Psychoanalytic Psychotherapy, the faculty of the Institute for the Advancement of Self Psychology, and the Advisory Board of the International Association for Relational Psychoanalysis and Psychotherapy. His many contributions have been honored by the Ontario Psychological Association, the American Psychological Association, the Canadian Psychological Association, the International Federation for Psychoanalytic Education, the University of Chicago, the Chicago Institute for Psychoanalysis, and the National Association for the Advancement of Psychoanalysis.

REFERENCES

American Academy of Sleep Medicine. (2005). The International classification of sleep disorders: diagnostic and coding manual, 3rd. Edition. Westchester, Ill: American Academy of Sleep Medicine.

Attarian, H.P. (2010). A terrified and terrifying scream. In A. Culebras: *Case Studies in Sleep Neurology: Common and Uncommon Presentations*. Cambridge: Cambridge University Press, pp. 110-116.

Bennett, D. (2011). The minds of sleepwalking killers. *Science Focus: The Online Home of BBC Focus Magazine*, March 10.

Bion, W.R. (1980). *Bion in New York and Sao Paulo*. F. Bion (Ed.). Strath Tay: Clunie Press.

Britton, R. (1989). The missing link: Parental sexuality in the Oedipus complex. In J. Steiner (Ed.), The Oedipus complex today: Clinical implications. London: Karnac Books.

Brogaard, B. & Marlow, K. (2012). Sleep driving and sleep killing: The Kenneth Parks case. *Psychology Today*, Dec. 13. https://www.psychologytoday.com/us/blog/the-superhuman-mind/201212/sleep-driving-and-sleep-killing.

Broughton, R. (1968). Sleep disorders: Disorders of arousal? *Science*, 159:1070-1078.

Broughton, R., Billings, R., Cartwright, R., Doucette, D., Edmeads, J., Edwardh, M., Ervin, F., Orchard, B., Hill, R., Turrell, G. (1994). Homicidal somnambulism: a case report. *Sleep*, 17(3):253-64.

Callwood, J. (1990). *The Sleepwalker*. Toronto: Lester & Orpen Dennys.

Carlin, J. (2014). *Chase Your Shadow: The Trials of Oscar Pistorius*. London: Atlantic Books.

Carpenter, S. (2001). Sights unseen. *Monitor on Psychology*. April, pp. 54-57.

Cartwright, R.D. (2010). *The Twenty-Four Hour Mind: The Role of Sleep and Dreaming in our Emotional Lives*. Oxford & New York: Oxford University Press.

Cramer Bornemann, M.A. & Mahowald, M.W. (2017). Sleep Forensics: Criminal Culpability for Sleep-Related Violence. In: M. H. Kryger, T. Roth & W. C. Dement (Eds.), *Principles and Practice of Sleep Medicine* (Sixth Edition). Philadelphia: Elsevier, pp. 653-660.

Denno, D.W. (2002). Crime and consciousness: Science and involuntary acts. *Minnesota Law Review*, 87(2): 369-400.

Ekirch, A.R. (2010). Violence in the Land of Sleep. *New York Times,* March 23.

Fantini, M.L., Corona, A., Clerici, S., & Ferini-Strambi, L. (2005). Aggressive dream content without without daytime aggressiveness in REM sleep behavior disorder. *Neurology*, 65:1010-1015.

Ferguson, M. & Taylor, P. (2014). *Oscar: An Accident Waiting to Happen*. MF Books.

Freud, S. (1915). Thoughts for the times on war and death. *The Standard Edition of the Complete Psychological Works of Sigmund Freud,* 14: 273-300.

Gannon, K. (2016). A nation divided by love and honour. *Toronto Star,* July 16, p. IN8.

Gastaut, H. & Broughton, R. (1965). A clinical and polygraphic study of episodic phenomena during sleep. In J. Wortis (Ed.), *Recent Advances in Biological Psychiatry,* 7:197-221. New York: Plenum.

Green, A. (1986). The dead mother. In K. Aubertin (translator): *On Private Madness.* London: Hogarth Press, pp. 142-173.

Guilleminault, C., Kirisoglu, C., Bao, G., Arias, V., Chan, A., & Li, K.K. (1995). Forensic sleep medicine: nocturnal wandering and violence. *Sleep,* 18:740-748.

Kleitman, N. (1963). *Sleep and Wakefulness,* revised and enlarged edition. Chicago: University of Chicago Press.

Mack, A. & Rock, I. (1998). *Inattentional Blindness.* Cambridge, MA: MIT Press.

Mahowald, M.W., Schenck, C.H., Cramer Bornemann, M.A. (2011). Violent parasomnias: forensic implications. In: P. Montagna & S. Chokroverty (Editors), *Handbook of Clinical Neurology.* Amsterdam: Elsevier, pp. 1149-1159.

Moldofsky, H., Gilbert, R., Lue, F.A., MacLean, A.W. (1995). Forensic sleep medicine: Sleep-related violence. *Sleep,* 18:731-739.

Pressman, M.R. (2007). Disorders of arousal and violence: Role of physical provocation and proximity. *Sleep,* 30(8): 1038-1047.

Pressman, M.R. & Broughton, R. (2015). NREM arousal parasomnias. In S. Chokroverty & M. Billiard (Eds.), *Sleep Medicine: A Comprehensive Guide to its Development, Clinical Milestones, and Advances in Treatment.* New York: Springer, pp. 375-389.

Randall, D.K. (2012). *Dreamland: Adventures in the Strange Science of Sleep.* New York: Norton.

Rubin, P. (1999). Wake-Up Call. *Phoenix New Times,* July 1. *http://www.phoenixnewtimes.com/news/wake-up-call-6421198.*

Schenck, C.H. (2005). *Paradox Lost: Midnight in the Battleground of Sleep and Dreams.* Extreme Nights, LLC.

_____ (2007). *Sleep: A Groundbreaking Guide to the Mysteries, the Problems, and the Solutions.* New York: Penguin.

Schenck, C.H., Boyd, J.L., & Mahowald, M.W. (1997). A parasomnia overlap disorder involving sleepwalking, sleep terrors, and REM sleep behavior disorder in 33 polysomnographically confirmed cases. *Sleep,* 20 (11):972-981.

Schenck, C.H., Lee, S.A., Cramer Bornemann, M.A., & Mahowald, M.W. (2009). Potentially lethal behaviors associated with rapid eye movement sleep behavior disorder: Review of the literature and forensic implications. *Journal of Forensic Sciences,* 54(6):1475-1484.

Seal, M. (2013). The shooting star and the model. *Vanity Fair.* May 14 (online).

Siclari, F., Khalami, R., Urbanick, F., Nobili, L., Mahowald, M.H., Schenck, C.H., Cramer Bornemann, M.A. (2010). Violence in sleep. *Brain,* 133(12):3494-3509.

Simons, D. & Chabris, C. (1999). Gorillas in our midst: sustained inattentional blindness for dynamic events. *Perception*, 28: 1059-1074.

Steenkamp, J. (2014). *Reeva: A Mother's Story.* Sphere (Little, Brown Book Group Limited): 2015.

Wiener, M. & Bateman, B. (2014). *One Tragic Night.* New York: St. Martin's Press.

Wilsons, Jade. Oscar Pistorius hospitalized after throwing himself off a prison bunk bed, haunted by Reeva. *Gossip Mill Mzansi.*